Muslims

Beliefs, Customs and Traditions

Sayyed Abul Hasan 'Ali Nadwi

UK ISLAMIC ACADEMY

ISBN 1 872531 74 1 (PB)

Translator: Muhyiddin Ahmad

General Editor: Iqbal Ahmad Azami

Published by

UK Islamic Academy
PO Box 6645
Leicester LE5 5WT
United Kingdom

Website: www.ukiabooks.com
E-mail: info@ukiabooks.com

British Library Cataloguing in Publication Data

A catalogue record for this book is available from the British Library

Design and Typeset by Muhammad al-Madani

CONTENTS

بسم الله الرحمن الرحيم

In the name of Allah, Most Gracious, Most Merciful

Foreword

Islam and Muslims are so frequently misunderstood and misrepresented in the West that any work which seeks to correct this is an asset in itself. So much anti-Islamic rhetoric is heard these days, not least because of poor and incorrect media coverage of concepts such as *jihad*, construed as holy war but actually meaning striving in the way of Islam including where necessary defence of the faith, that there is little wonder that Islam is feared as something of a menace and a disturbing influence to be arrested.

Originally published in India to assist Hindus particularly, as also Jains and Buddhists, gain a better understanding of Muslims, *Muslims: Beliefs, Customs and Traditions* is now being made available to a Western audience in order to fulfil the same requirement. Although this first British edition has been revised and improved with the addition of a Glossary and an Index, the substance of Sayyed Abul Hasan 'Ali Nadwi's work remains unchanged. The essence of what he imparts to us has always been and will always be the true spirit of Islam.

In its fluent, accessible style this book covers all the facets of a Muslim's everyday life, from birth through education, marriage and death. Additionally, all obligatory and voluntary religious observances are detailed in the exact manner in which they are performed. This is not a work of propaganda or faith-bashing but rather a genuine attempt to present the life of a Muslim as it really is. In so doing, it is also a useful asset to Muslims themselves, an *aide-memoire* of what is expected of them as Believers.

Especially enlightening are those sections of the work which describe in detail the observances and festivals of *Ramadan*, and the requirements made of pilgrims to Makkah. Of similar merit are the descriptions of those ceremonies, customs and festivals of a purely Indian Muslim origin, for example the slight variations practiced in marriage contracts and ceremonies.

Whether you are a Believer or a non-Believer, whether you are a Muslim, Christian, Jew, Hindu or Buddhist, this is an indispensable introduction to the ways and practices of Islam. In this relatively short work much ignorance and hearsay about a faith, Islam, which is more often than not misrepresented and misunderstood is dispelled.

I would like to thank Susan Thackeray, my son Muhammad Madani, my daughters Su'ad and Asma and all those who have participated in the production of this volume. May Allah reward all of them and accept this work from us and make it a source of guidance for Muslims the world over. To Allah belongs all good, and by His favours all righteous deeds come into existence.

Leicester (England) **Iqbal Ahmad Azami**
Sha'bān 1426 / September 2005

Introduction

Muslims and non-Muslims have lived together in India for a thousand years. In every city, town and village they are not only neighbours, they are also colleagues and partners in businesses and trades, schools and offices. They have also jointly participated in movements launched for the liberation of the country from foreign rule, and are still co-workers in different political and social organisations; on the railways and in the buses they can be seen travelling together; but, it is an incomprehensible mystery that they are not even as much acquainted with each other's religious beliefs, customs, traditions and cultures as people belonging to two different lands. What they do know about each other is more often than not a jumble of tittle-tattle and misconceived notions, hearsay and prejudices. Naturally such a distorted view, aided and abetted by the malice and prejudice of sectarian propaganda gimmicks and distorted history textbooks is bound to produce a perverse and grotesque picture of the other community. The careless glance which men of culture and learning condescend to cast on the basic tenets and beliefs, manners and morals of the other community serves only to confirm the ignorance if not the prejudice harboured by misguided fanatics. Not unoften the opinions expressed by fairly educated persons about the faith and customs of the other community have to be dismissed with a laugh. The impression gained by the writer of these lines is always confirmed by conversations with people from every walk of life whom he comes across, during the journeys frequently undertaken by him.

Yet this is not a matter to be laughed away. We have been living together for hundreds of years but we are still so ignorant of each other. The responsibility for this does not lie with any particular community; it devolves on both and, particularly, on those who claim to be religious and social workers, patriots and philanthropists. It is they who have as yet made no sincere effort to diffuse correct and unbiased information about the two communities; whatever effort they did make in the past has been inadequate and half-hearted. It has now been accepted that co-operation, peace and amity between the two peoples cannot be obtained without a true understanding of each other's religion and culture: every group, faction and community comprising the nation has, of necessity, to know the beliefs, customs, traditions, observances and taboos of the other people. One has to understand what are the dominant traits or the cultural patterns of another community, what are the social, spiritual, and moral values, beliefs and tenets dearer to them than their own life and progeny. One has to understand what they need to lead a contented and peaceful existence, and what their inherent predilections, inner streaks of mind and heart, temperaments and dispositions are which have to be taken into consideration for any purposeful dialogue with them. These are the prerequisites of peaceful coexistence between different communities living anywhere, but more so in a country which has for so long taken pride in its charming variety of creeds and cultures and which has always upheld the principle of Live And Let Live. There is a general tendency nowadays to acquire knowledge about the religions and philosophies, cultures and customs, languages and literatures, habits and hobbies of people living in far-off lands; universities offer special courses on these subjects; cultural delegations are exchanged and students are encouraged to pursue further studies abroad; but the two peoples living in India, Hindus and Muslims, are still as ignorant of each other as are people living in two different countries.

The situation obtaining in this regard is equally harmful to the Muslims as well as to the Hindus and, in the final analysis, to the country and even humanity at large. A deep gulf of prejudice and suspicion divides the two communities; misunderstanding, distrust and prejudice against one another embitters their relations; friendliness and companionship are foreign to them while they lack a genuine understanding, tolerance and respect for the creed and culture of the other. The country suffers, obviously, as a consequence. In these circumstances minorities, especially the Muslims, consider it their duty to preserve and protect their religion, culture and language. Their redoubtable capabilities which have left indelible imprints of their achievements in almost every field – from philosophy and mysticism to architecture and fine arts and from the governance of the country to the common weal of the people – are not being directed to the extent they should have been for the reconstruction and development of the country. Psychologically speaking too, they need reassurance that they are not being misunderstood, that they are relied upon and respected by their sister communities. They have to know that no veil of distrust intervenes between them and the majority community, nor are they looked upon with suspicion and hatred or with a feeling of estrangement. Such a sense of security can only be produced by an awareness that the sister communities, with whom they have been living for a thousand years, know them adequately, their merits and failings, their past and present, their creed, culture, customs, observances, rites and festivals. The same applies to the Muslims. Their knowledge of Hindus has, of necessity, to be more profound and intimate than that possessed by any other people.

A number of works, written by Muslims as well as non-Muslims, describing the attainments of the Muslim era, the efforts made by

Muslims to give a clean and stable administration to India, to make her strong and great, their cultural heritage and their contribution to the arts and literature of the country, already exist. The author of these lines too penned a book entitled *Muslims in India* which has since been published in Arabic, Urdu and English.* All these works, however, fall within the scope of history and are of interest to students of history and research scholars.

The real need of the hour is for a book dealing with the present rather than with the past. Apart from what the Muslims have been in bygone days, the immediate need is to depict the life of present-day Muslims – what they now are, irrespective of any consideration of whether this is liked by anyone or not. The endeavour should aim to depict present-day Muslims in India without magnifying or concealing any facet of their life or without giving vent to one's own preferences or prejudices. Such a picture should be a study in still life – a portraiture of life seen through a photograph rather than a decorative painting. It should be factual, neither contentious nor argumentative. I do not mean to say that putting forth one's own point of view or the airing of one's creed or philosophy is something undesirable, but a work designed to portray the life of Muslims should better be strictly informative. We already have a good number of such books on Islam as, for example, *Road to Makkah* by Muhammad Asad (formerly Leopold Weiss), *Towards Understanding Islam* by Maulana

* The Arabic version is entitled *al-Muslimoona fil-Hind* and the Urdu version *Hindustani Musalman*. A series of lectures delivered by the author on All India Radio in 1951, after his return from a tour of Middle Eastern countries acquainting the Arabs with the achievements of Indian Muslims, were published in a book produced in Damascus. Its Urdu and English versions were later brought out by the Academy of Islamic Research and Publications, Lucknow.

Sayyed Abul Ala Maududi, *Introduction to Islam* by Dr. Hamidullah and *What Islam Is* by Maulana Muhammad Manzoor No'mani. These books can easily be had from any library by those who are interested in the study of Islam. Unlike these books, the present work is intended to be an informative book of common interest, written in a simple and unaffected style portraying the present-day life of Indian Muslims. Not designed to cater for erudite and philosophic minds, it is meant for those average educated non-Muslims who could not for whatever reason acquaint themselves with the way of life of their Muslim brethren, but who now need knowledge of it for satisfactorily discharging their day-to-day duties, such as in journalism or for carrying out political or social work. I hope this book will be found helpful by them not only in their daily business but also as an incentive for further studies on the subject.

In this book I have kept in mind the *Ahl-i-Sunnat wal Jama'at*, commonly known as *Sunnis*, to which belong the overwhelming majority of Indian Muslims. This is not because other Indian Muslim sects do not deserve mention, but that I can only authoritatively speak on behalf of my own sect, i.e. the *Sunnis*. In other words, I think myself morally bound to present their way of life as best I can. A similar effort on my part on behalf of other sects would be fraught with the danger of misrepresentation, however unintentional. Then, there is also no dearth of savants and writers of repute among the other communities of Indian Muslims. I would, therefore, earnestly advise them to pen similar tracts depicting the life of their own brethren. I have, nevertheless, mentioned, wherever absolutely necessary, the differences and distinguishing features of the second largest community among the Indian Muslims, i.e. the *Ithna 'Ashari* sect or the Shi'ahs as they are commonly known. If these descriptions are somewhat sketchy, I regret the same but no more space could be devoted to the description of these differing characteristics in this slim volume.

Given that the purpose of this book is to present the manners and customs, observances and way of thinking of Indian Muslims, the corresponding features of the lives of Muslims in other countries have not been delineated here. However, Islam is a universal religion rooted in the Qur'an and the *Sunnah*, and, therefore, there is hardly any difference in the basic tenets and religious observances of the Muslims of other countries. Indian Muslims have, on the other hand, adopted numerous customs and usages of the land which have been pointed out where necessary in order to identify their indigenous origin.

Furthermore, I have not made a point of suppressing my own ideas, feelings and predictions for this would have reflected an artificial treatment of the subject or, to put it more bluntly, such an endeavour would have been simply hypocritical. Any such effort would have made my writing lifeless and as dry as dust. I have, nevertheless, tried to be moderate in expressing my own views on any subject and avoided all references which could even faintly be construed as aggressive or offensive to anyone. Although I lay no claim to any erudition in writing these pages, still, I am satisfied that this publication may be a humble service to my nation and homeland.

I sincerely wish that similar informative books written in an easy and simple style, avoiding philosophical and controversial issues, be published about the life and culture of other communities, particularly the majority community of India. The ignorance of Muslims about the manners and morals of Hindus, or, for that matter, of other castes and creeds is as bad as that of non-Muslims about their Muslim brethren. Hindus and Muslims both, therefore, have to give attention to this urgent task. Having performed what I consider to be my duty on behalf of Indian Muslims, I hope that our non-Muslim friends will soon come forward to help root out present feelings of alienation and estrangement which are largely a product of ignorance about the way of living and thinking of the different communities of this subcontinent. At least this blind and dark ignorance should not be allowed to disrupt brotherly relations between the different castes, creeds and communities of our great country.

Daira Shah 'Alamullah **Abul Hasan Ali Nadwi**
Rae Bareli

I

FROM BIRTH TO ADULTHOOD

Birth of the Child

When a baby is born in a Muslim family, he is first taken to an elder and pious member of the family or a neighbour who whispers the words of the *adhan*[1] into the baby's right ear, and those of the *iqamah* into his left ear. The *adhan* and *iqamah* are essential prerequisites of the Muslim Prayer. The baby, obviously, is completely unaware of this ceremonial chanting but the intention is that the first thing he should hear is the name of God and the Muslim confession of faith. It is also customary on this occasion to place a small piece of date chewed by some pious person into the baby's mouth. This custom, which has the sanction of Prophetic tradition, is intended to sanctify the newly-born child.

The birth of a baby is, for the Muslim family, a joyful event; the occasion being enlivened by differing customs and ceremonies depending more often on local traditions and the social and economic status of the family. Greetings are exchanged between the relatives who wish good luck to the parents. Another custom peculiar to Indian Muslims but not prevalent among Arabs or Muslims elsewhere is the presentation of garments or other articles of clothing for the baby by the near relatives, especially from the mother's side. This custom varies slightly in different parts of the country.

'Aqiqah of the Child

The birth of the baby is celebrated by shaving the baby's head and by offering a living sacrifice. The ceremony, known as *'aqiqah*, is normally performed on the seventh day after the child's birth.[2] If for any reason it is not performed on the seventh day it can be carried out on the fourteenth or a subsequent day fixed in this manner. Two goats are sacrificed if the infant is a male, otherwise one is considered sufficient. The flesh is given to the poor and is also distributed among relatives. There is no bar to its consumption by family members and relatives who are often invited to partake of the meal at the house of the parents. The *aqiqah* is, however, neither obligatory (*fard*) nor essential (*wajib*), nor is the sacrifice a duty incumbent on the parents. Therefore, one can forgo the ceremony if one's means do not permit it.

The usage common among Indian Muslims is to invite relatives and friends on the day appointed for the *'aqiqah*. The barber is then called who ceremoniously removes the baby's hair. Alms are then given in the form of a quantity of silver equal to the weight of the baby's hair or its approximate price. This practice is followed to emulate the Prophet of Islam (peace be upon him) who is reported to have distributed alms in a similar manner. In certain sections of Muslims, the family barber, who belongs to one of the serving castes and is attached to the higher-cum-feudal classes, performs *'aqiqah* and other similar ceremonial functions. On the joyous occasion of *'aqiqah* as well as on occasions of a similar nature the family barber receives rewards throughout the ceremony, on different pretexts, from members of the household and their near kin, and this constitutes a major source of his income.

Naming the Child

The infant is normally given a name on the occasion of *'aqiqah*, and it is more often proposed by an elder member of the family or a neighbour revered for his piety. Sometimes the parents or members of the family themselves select a suitable name for the child. Indian Muslims prefer to give their children Arabic names; or, more correctly, like Muslims elsewhere, names expressing an Islamic denomination are adopted so that there may be no doubt about the child's religion. Muslim doctors of faith consider the practice beneficial from a psychological view-point and insist on it for maintaining the religious identity of the Muslims. They look with disfavour upon the practice followed by Chinese Muslims whose names give no indication of whether one is a Muslim or not. There are, however, no religious injunctions which call upon Muslims to give any particular type of name to their child except that such names are preferred which are expressive of the Unity of God and submission to Him. A great majority of Muslim names in India and other countries, therefore, contain that which has '*abd* (slave) as a prefix of one of the Divine attributes,[3] such as 'Abdullah, 'Abdur Rahman, 'Abdul Wāhid, 'Abdul Aḥad, 'Abduṣ-Ṣamad, 'Abdul 'Aziz, 'Abdul Mājid, 'Abdul Majeed and so on. At the same time, it is exceptionable to have names which smack of pride or disobedience. Names such as *Malik-ul-Muluk* (King of Kings), or *Shahenshah* (Emperor) are accordingly viewed with disfavour.

Names of the Prophets and Companions

In giving names to their children, the Muslims' second preference is for the names of their beloved Prophet (peace be upon him), his distinguished Companions and members of the Prophet's family. Another reason for the adoption of these names is to bless and sanctify the baby. In India, names which have Muhammad or Ahmad as one of their component parts abound; sometimes both these names of the Prophet are given to a child who is thus called Muhammad Ahmad; or else they prefer to have Muhammad as an essential prefix even though the child may not have been formally given that name on the occasion of *'aqiqah*. We, therefore, frequently come across such names as Muhammad Sa'eed, Muhammad 'Aziz, Muhammad Husain and the like. Other names commonly adopted are those of the Prophet's family and his Companions. Daughters usually receive the names of the wives and daughters of the Prophet (peace be upon him).

An interesting feature of Muslim names is that the Prophet of Islam (peace be upon him) belonged to the Ismaelite branch of the Semitic race with whom the Muslims have always had a religious and emotional attachment. However, among the descendants of Shem the Israelites and Ismaelites have had a long-standing feud which continues even to present times in the shape of differences between the Jews and the Arabs. This bitterness, however, has never led Muslims to avoid the names of the Israelite Prophets. The Muslim creed of having faith in the prophethood of every Apostle sent by God for the guidance of humanity has saved them from falling prey to the racial prejudice normally engendered by the centuries-old enmity and hatred between the two nations. There are hundreds of thousands of Muslims in India, as in Arab countries and the rest of the Muslim world, who have been named after the Prophet Is'haq[4] (Isaac) and his descendants, such as Yaqoob (Jacob), Yusuf (Joseph), Da'ud (David), Sulaiman (Solomon), Musa (Moses), Haroon (Aaron), 'Isa (Jesus), Zakariyya (Zechariah), Yahya (John) (peace be upon them) among the males and Maryam (Mary), Safura (Sapphira), and similar other names among women.

Some Undesirable Names

Indian Muslims have also evolved certain names which are peculiar to them indicating either a local personality cult or an undue veneration of the saints. Some such common names found among Indian Muslims often run counter to their belief in the Unity and Overlordship of God. One of the foremost articles of the Islamic faith is that God alone is the Provider of sustenance, Bestower of children and the Forgiver of sins, but quite a number of Indian Muslim names ascribe these Divine attributes to the saints and venerated personages belonging to the Prophet's household (peace be upon him). Some such undesirable names include Salar Bakhsh, Madar Bakhsh, Qalandar Bakhsh, Sabir Bakhsh, 'Ali Bakhsh, Husain Bakhsh, 'Abdul Husain,[5] etc.

Another significant feature of Indian Muslim names is that they are usually composed of two different elements as, for example, Muhammad Hasan, Mahmood Hasan, Usman Ahmad, Ali Murtaza, while the Arabs prefer single names. Wherever the Arabs have composite names, the first name is the original name of the man while the subsequent part indicates the name of his father, the family name or the *laqab* (surname). In Gujrat, Maharashtra and certain southern states of India, Muslims have their first names completed by the addition of their father's names. There are also certain common surnames among Hindus as well as Muslims in certain southern parts of the country, such as Deshmukh, Modak, Tankar, etc. which denote either the ancestral village or town or the occupation or office held by one's forefathers under the Indian princes before establishment of British rule in India.

Names of Indian Origin and Aliases

In India there are also names of a purely Indian origin. One or both portions of such names, normally composite ones, are derived from Urdu, Persian or one of the local dialects, and are easily distinguished from the more common Islamic names of Indian Muslims. Such composite names include Bunyad Husain, Gulzar 'Ali, Allah Diya, Barkhurdar, 'Umar Daraz Beg. There are still other purely indigenous names, such as Hubdar Khan, Umrao Mirza, Amir Baz Khan, Baz Mir, which are not found anywhere else nor is it possible to say how these have come into vogue in certain areas.

Besides the proper name given to a man, there is also the custom of having an alias, by which one is called by friends and relatives. Sometimes, however, a person's alternative name becomes so well known that even his intimate friends do not know his original name. These aliases are very often given either as pet names to children to be used in familiar affection or are abbreviations of longer names. Aliases are more commonly used in Oudh, particularly around Lucknow. Such names include Naushah Mian, Piare Mian, Basawan Mian, Banney Mian, Ji Mian, Naqqan Sahib, Kabban Sahib, and the like.

Circumcision

Another ritual following the Abrahamic tradition that a child has to undergo after *'aqiqah* is circumcision or *khatnah*. The Arabs have always observed the ceremony of *khatnah* and it was also the practice followed by the Prophet of Islam (peace be upon him). Normally, the operation is performed by a barber but nowadays people have the circumcision operation performed in hospital where better medical facilities are available. This is also regarded as a festive occasion for the family when friends and relatives are invited to participate in the joyous event.

The Ceremony of *Bismillah*

Soon after a child is able to speak and comprehend things an elderly and pious person is invited to initiate the instruction of the child. This ceremony, known as *Bismillah*, marks the beginning of the child's education. In families which are economically well-off it is a festive occasion celebrated with pride and pomp. Also known as *tasmia khwani*[6] and *maktab nashini*,[7] the ceremony is, at places, performed when the child attains the age of four years, four months and four days. It is difficult to ascertain if the age fixed for the ceremony has any numerical significance or how it originated, but it definitely has no religious sanction.

The teacher performing the initiation ceremony first asks the child to repeat *Bismillah-ir-Rahman-ir-Rahim* (in the name of Allah the Beneficent, the Merciful) and then, after praying to God to bless the child with light and learning, formally teaches a few words from a primer of the Qur'an. In India, the preparatory textbook normally used on this occasion is *Qa'ida Baghdadhi*. When the ceremony is over, all those present invoke the blessings of God for the child, then sweets are distributed and the guests entertained with light refreshments.

Beginning the Teaching of the Qur'an

Besides *tasmia khwani*, there are two more ceremonies relating to the education of the child, which are now seldom performed owing to the changed curriculum and education system. The first of these is gone through when the child begins reading the Qur'an. On this occasion, those five verses of the Qur'an which were first revealed to the Prophet (peace be upon him) and are very meaningful and suited to the occasion, are repeated by the child. These are:

> *"In the name of Allah, the Beneficent, the Merciful.*
> *Read: (O Muhammad), In the name of thy Lord Who createth,*
> *Createth man from a clot.*

Read: And thy Lord is the Most Bounteous
Who teacheth by the pen.
Teacheth man that which he knew not." (Al-'Alaq 96: 1–5).

Completion of the Qur'an

The second function pertaining to the education of the child is observed when the child has read the entire Qur'an. This is normally a simple ceremony when sweets are distributed or sherbet is served to those present, and a presentation of garments is made to the teacher. In certain places, it is also customary to reward the teacher with cash. This ceremony is known as *nashrah.*

Instruction in Cleanliness and Purification

Children are taught, from the tender age when they begin to speak, to keep their body and clothes clean from dirt and all other impurities. Later on, when they begin formal education, they are encouraged to wash their private parts with water after urination and excretion. Insistence on a child's ritual purification by educated parents serves to instil a sense of cleanliness in the child. This also, however, depends on the surroundings, occupation of the parents and the instruction of the child by its teachers. Parents with a religious bent of mind are generally more scrupulous in this regard.

Instruction to Offer *Salat*

Children are also taught how to perform *wudu'*, i.e. the ritual ablution necessary for offering Prayers. Boys are encouraged from an early age to accompany their fathers while going to the mosque for Prayers. This offers them an opportunity to learn how to perform the Prayers and also to cultivate the habit of doing so.

A tradition of the Prophet (peace be upon him) directs that the child be instructed to offer Prayers when he attains the age of seven years and he is admonished for it if he is not accustomed to it by the age of ten.

Coaching in Etiquette and Manners

In Muslim society, young children are more the responsibility of their mothers than any other member of the family. Educated and cultured mothers always keep an eye on the manners of their children and teach them the rules of courtesy and good behaviour as dictated by religious precepts. Children are taught to begin every good work as, for example, taking water and food or shaking hands, with the right hand and cleansing the private parts with the left one. They are urged to sit down while taking water and to drink it in three breaths. They are trained to salute their elders first; say *Alhamdu lillah* whenever they sneeze; begin taking food with *Bismillah* and offer thanks to God after their meals. Mothers normally ensure that youngsters commit to memory some of the smaller chapters of the Qur'an and also other supplications of daily use. Mothers also try to infuse the spirit of true faith, righteousness and dutifulness into their children through fables and stories of the Prophets and the events related by them from the history of Islam. The constant aim of every well-bred Muslim mother is to make her child virtuous and upright, a believing Muslim and an ideal person. In fact, the importance attached to the family in Islam arises from the duty of the parents to provide instruction to the child not only in what are known as the rights of God, i.e. religious observances and behaviour in conformity with the norms of morality and religion but also good manners, especially in matters of etiquette and politeness, and the rights of one's fellow-beings, for all these form part of the Muslims' faith in Islam.

The Fast-breaking Ceremony

Rozah, also known as *saum,* is enjoined by the religious law of Islam as an obligatory observance on every Muslim, but, on condition that he is an adult and in sound physical and mental health. However, infatuated with enthusiasm to emulate their parents and relatives young boys and girls insist on keeping fasts along with elder members of the family. Young boys often begin observing the fast secretly or are encouraged by their parents to keep their first fast (*rozah*) at the age of about ten or eleven years. This also being an occasion for family rejoicing, relatives and friends as well as the child's friends keeping the fast are invited to a special feast. The ceremony, called *rozah kusha'i,* provides another occasion for elaborate preparations being made for the fast-breaking meal, or *iftari,* which is taken just after sunset. Even people not in possession of a moderately good income deem it necessary to make special arrangements for such feasts. The ceremony has, in certain places, gradually assumed sufficient importance that the feast attended by friends and relatives is its central function.

The two essential religious observances, Prayer and fasting, become obligatory on all adults possessing mental and physical faculties and, on the fulfilment of certain other conditions elaborated in the law books; they are required to undertake the pilgrimage to Makkah (*hajj*) and pay the poor-due (*zakat*). Attainment of the age of majority[8] thus brings a Muslim under the operation of the laws prescribing permissible and prohibited acts, holds him responsible for his omissions and commissions and renders him liable to punishment in the Hereafter for any disregard of Divine injunctions.

NOTES

1. For an explanation of these terms, see Chapter V, relating to Religious Observances.

2. The seventh day performance of *'aqiqah* is *mustahab*, i.e. it is a meritorious act which can earn reward in the Hereafter but the omission of it does not expose one to any punishment.
3. The second part of these names denotes the adjectival names of God, as, for example, *Raḥman* (The Most Compassionate), *Waḥeed* (The Lonely), *Wāhid* (The One), *Aḥad* (The One), *Ṣamad* (The Eternally Besought of all), etc.
4. The Prophet and progenitor of the Israelites, was the step-brother of Ismael, the ancestor of the Arabs.
5. A number of eminent doctors of faith vehemently object to such names which they consider as un-Islamic. One of the most respected reformers and defenders of Islam in India, Maulana Sayyed Ahmad Shahid Barelwi (d. 1246/1830) changed thousands of such names during his extensive travels undertaken for the spiritual and moral uplift of his co-religionists. (See *Sayyed Ahmad Shahid* by Muhyiddin Ahmad, for the great reformative endeavour of the 19th Century in India, published by the Academy of Islamic Research and Publications, Lucknow).
6. Recitation of the name of God.
7. Admission to a seminary.
8. For the performance of religious observances, the legal age of majority is 15 years.

II

FROM ADULTHOOD TO DEATH

Marriage is not only a social necessity and a commendable act in the eyes of the religious canon (*Shari'ah*), it is also a major landmark in the life of a Muslim attaining manhood. Islam does not view with favour any undue delay, unless there are some cogent reasons for it, in the marriage of a Muslim after attaining the permissible age; in this way, it seeks to close the door on immorality and dissoluteness. The religious law of Islam does not prescribe any particular age for contracting marriage, the marriageable age depends on the general physique of a man, his upbringing and circumstances as well as the climatic conditions and customs obtaining in a particular country. It only enjoins that one should enter into wedlock soon after attaining puberty.

Indian Customs adopted by Muslims

The democratic structure of the Islamic social order still in vogue in other Islamic countries, particularly in Arabic-speaking lands, has been gradually given up by Indian Muslims who are guided in establishing matrimonial relationships by considerations of caste and family. Preference is given here to the spouse belonging to one's own caste, and within the same caste, to a consort of the same family. This bespeaks of a leaning for racial or blood relationship which is sometimes absurdly insisted upon in the matrimonial union. This obviously owes its origin to the Indian caste system or social stratification among the sister community,[1] which has so long been scrupulously adhered to by them. In comparison to Indian Muslims, whose social structure has become a victim of caste discrimination, their co-religionists in other countries appear to be more broadminded and unfettered by the shackles of custom and ritual. In establishing matrimonial relationships, Muslims of other countries take into account the social, economic and educational status of the spouses – any marked disparity being looked upon with disfavour, but the Indian Muslim communities arrogating themselves as *ashraf* or *shurafaa*[2] consider it absolutely essential to unite in marriage only those who descend from a common progenitor. They overlook the social and moral evils which are produced by such a strict adherence to social stratification, and have sometimes to pay dearly for this. The changing social order, economic pressures and the wide diffusion of education among the masses are slowly bringing about a change in the outlook of the people; now greater preference is being given to the economic status, education and the good looks of the couple. This is, of course, a novel experience for the Muslim community as a whole, one which is sometimes successful and at times ends in failure; but, be this as it may, considerations of caste and consanguine relations are increasingly being relegated to a lower priority.

Marriages within the Family Circle

Contrary to the Hindu custom of solemnising marriages outside the family circle, Indian Muslims prefer to intermarry within the family, barring, of course, the prohibited degrees of relationships.[3] In certain families, marriages between cousins, i.e. the sons or daughters of an uncle or aunt, are given preference over other matches, although the practice is now losing ground owing to a variety of reasons.

The Marriage Proposal

There is not much difference between the way marriage proposals are finalised and various other rites in vogue connected with the formal declaration of such an engagement amongst Hindus and Muslims. These rites also differ from place to place but the observance of local customs and rituals amongst Muslims, particularly in educated and well-to-do families, is not as punctilious as amongst the majority community. On the whole, these observances are on the decline owing to the influence of modern education.

The Islamic Way of Marriage

Islam looks upon the *nikah* (the contract of marriage) and the connected functions generally known as *shadi* as an austere and simple affair. It is, in its view, a social necessity which should be solemnly observed like an act of worship. Muslim law lays down no specific religious ceremony, nor any religious rituals necessary for the contraction of a valid marriage. Legally, a marriage contracted between two persons possessing the capacity to enter into the contract is valid and binding, if entered into by mutual consent in the presence of two witnesses. Its only aim is to declare that the couple are not being united in wedlock secretly or surreptitiously but with the knowledge of all concerned. Islam also enjoins the husband to pay the *mahr* or the dower-money to his wife, treat her with kindness and undertake to support and maintain her in a way suitable to his own means and position in society. These stipulations cover the injunctions laid down by Islam for the contraction of marriage: no more rites or customs were considered necessary or were in vogue in the early Muslim society. Numerous examples of frugal simplicity in marriages can be cited from the life of early precursors of Islam. Madinah had a slender population of Muslims after their migration from Makkah but we find a Companion of the Prophet (peace be upon him), who was closely related to him and had migrated with him from his ancestral city, contracting marriage without inviting the Prophet (peace be upon him) to attend the ceremony. The Prophet (peace be upon him) came to know of the marriage only later on.[4]

Ostentatious Celebration of Marriages

In India, as also in other Muslim countries, marriages have become occasions for festive rejoicing marked by rigid and costly ceremonial functions, and a means of ostentatious display of one's pride and opulence. The simplicity of the Islamic form of marriage has not been the only victim of these vain pretensions, it has also often brought in its train untold miseries to the families parading their grandiose nobility. Modern education and the economic regeneration of these countries has also been unable to change the current attitude or bring about any reform in these customs. Even in well-educated and religious-minded families elaborate arrangements are made for marriages, guests are entertained lavishly and the houses decorated colourfully. It is not unoften that entirely novel methods are adopted to flaunt the nobility and stateliness of the family and to make a show of its intimate connections with the ruling elite. The marriage is followed by a grand feast to celebrate the alliance, which again provides an occasion for the lavish entertainment of quite a large number of guests. The affair has become very costly, often requiring people to incur heavy debts in order to keep up appearances. These vain pretensions have given rise, not unexpectedly, to a contest in prodigal spending and a pompous show of false vanity and opulence. In this respect, Indian Muslims have left their co-religionists in other countries far behind in the festive celebration of marriages.

Music and Dancing

Except in families which strictly follow the rules of the *Shari'ah* or who are indoctrinated by religiously-oriented reformatory movements, marriage celebrations are invariably accompanied by musical sittings, dancing and amusements meant to entertain the guests. In such families, the marriage is preceded and followed by festive rejoicing; nautch girls and professional dancers belonging to servile classes are invited a few days before the function. In the performances held for the diversion of women the girls of the family also participate along with the dancing troupe. The bride is kept secluded, a few days before the marriage, and tradition demands that she observes *purdah* even from her nearest kin. Musical sittings are now often given over to the playing of recorded music. Dancing performances too, which were earlier considered an essential part of all festive rejoicing by feudal lords and grandees, are gradually being given up partly owing to economic pressures and partly because of modern education and the corrective influence of reformatory movements.

Local Customs in Muslim Marriages

Indian Muslims have adopted numerous rites and local customs which are not to be found among Muslims elsewhere. One of these customs relates to the demand known as *tilak* made by the bridegroom or his guardian, which has to be fulfilled by the parents of the bride. The custom is not prevalent everywhere in

India, nor among the Arabs or Turks who would find it difficult to understand its implications or the sense or spirit behind this seemingly senseless custom. It is not easy to describe the insurmountable difficulties and untold miseries caused by this custom and the obstacles placed by it in the way of finding a suitable match for marriageable girls in certain places. Similarly, the extensive and lavish arrangements made for marriage feasts are peculiar to Indian Muslims. The exhibition of *jahez*, the clothing, utensils and furniture given as a dowry to the bride by her parents, which are taken out in a procession, the rites of *ru-numai*, i.e. showing the face of the bride to the bridegroom after marriage, the *salaam* by the bridegroom, contributions by way of *neuta* by relatives, silly jokes exchanged by the in-laws, and the custom of ceremonial visits paid by the bride and the bridegroom to the house of the other, a ceremony known as *chauthi*, are some of the rites of indigenous origin unknown to the Muslims of other countries. All these rites and customs were perhaps the product of the concept commonly held that marriage is a festive occasion providing a temporary diversion from the cares and worries of daily life, when it is permissible to take leave of moral bindings and other serious pursuits in order to enjoy and amuse oneself. The idea, suited to local genus, also finds expression in the fairs and festivals of India, which have presented, from time immemorial, a fascinating spectacle of colourful celebration and an occasion for the reunion of friends and relatives.

The Performance of *Nikah*

Before the marital contract of *nikah* is solemnised, the bridegroom is dressed in new attire provided by the parents of the bride, and made to sit at a distinguished place in the gathering. In certain places, there is also the custom of dressing the bridegroom with a flowery veil (*sehra*) and brocade bracelets (*kangna*) which are, however, disliked by those who prefer to follow the precepts of religion. The *nikah* can be solemnised by any educated Muslim: it is not necessary that the person performing the ceremony should be a *Qazi*. In the bygone days of Muslim rule in India, the magistrates charged with the administration of justice or the Muslim legists, known as *Qazis*, performed this function also. It is, however, preferable under Islamic law that the father or the *Wali* (guardian)[5] of the bride should himself perform the ceremony as the Prophet of Islam (peace be upon him) himself solemnised the marriage of his daughter Fatimah with 'Ali. Before the ceremony of *nikah* is performed, an attorney and two witnesses who are more often near kin or members of the bride's family, repair to the girl to inform her of the marriage to be contracted in lieu of a stipulated dower and to seek her consent. In India, the bride usually keeps silent and this is taken as her tacit approval of the proposal made to her. The *Qazi* or the person performing the *nikah* then recites the *khutbah* in Arabic, consisting of a few verses of the Qur'an and the traditions of the Prophet (peace be upon him), and closes the discourse with an invocation of Divine blessings for the couple. Thereafter follows what is called *ijaab* and *qabool* or the offer and acceptance. Normally this consists of the proposal of marriage made to the bridegroom and his acceptance in these words: "Such as one's daughter, whose name is this, is given by me in marriage to you in lieu of such a dower settled on her; do you consent to it?" To this the bridegroom replies in a low but audible voice, "I consent." After this, the *Qazi* and all those present raise their hands to offer Prayers for mutual love and a successful married life for the couple. This invocation is also made in Arabic.

The Address of *Nikah*

The address delivered on the occasion of *nikah* is normally in Arabic but nowadays it is made up of the Qur'anic verses recited in Arabic followed by a speech in Urdu delineating the duties and obligations of the married couple. The *khutbah* is thus employed to instil a sense of responsibility in the bridegroom and to emphasise the moral-spiritual character of the *nikah* performed with the sanction of religion, and for the benefit of the audience.

Here we give a *khutbah* delivered on the occasion of marriage for the benefit of our readers. After repeating the supplications offered on such occasions by the Holy Prophet (peace be upon him), the *Qazi* continues:

> "I betake myself to Allah for refuge from the accursed Satan. (I begin) in the name of Allah the Beneficent, the Merciful.
> *O mankind; Be careful of your duty to your Lord.*
> *Who created you from a single soul and from it created its mate and from them twain hath spread abroad a multitude of men and women. Be careful of your duty toward Allah in Whom ye claim* (*your rights*) *of one another, and toward the wombs* (*that bare you*).
>
> *Lo: Allah hath been a Watcher over you.* (An-Nisā 4: 1).
>
> *O ye who believe; Observe your duty to Allah with right observance, and die not save as those who have surrendered* (unto Him). (Āl 'Imrān 3: 102).
>
> *O ye who believe; Guard your duty to Allah and speak words straight to the point; He will adjust your works for you and will forgive you your sins. Whosoever obeyth Allah and His Messenger, he verily hath gained a signal victory.*" (al-Aḥzāb 33: 70–1).
>
> "Gentlemen the *nikah* does not mean going through a ritual nor is it simply an act of worship or something having the concurrence of the Prophet (peace be upon him) alone. It is, in fact, an embodiment of several devotions, acts of

worship: not one, but numerous acts of oblation and offering, recognised as virtuous and holy, flow from it. It is a subject consecrated enough to be mentioned in the Glorious Qur'an and the traditions of the Holy Prophet; Islamic jurisprudence devotes a separate chapter to it; but alas, it is neglected by the people as no other *Sunnah*[6] of the Prophet has ever been ignored. Essentially, the *nikah* has become a means to flout the commandments of God, to obey the sneaking whispers of Satan and one's own longings and base desires; a lifeless ritual has it verily become. In truth, the *nikah* shows us how to lead a virtuous life. As you will have noted from the Qur'anic verses I have just recited and these were recited on similar occasions by the Prophet too – the most appropriate and propitious thing worth mentioning on this occasion is the genesis of the human race on this earth. It was the single soul of Adam from whom his mate was created, and then they filled this earth with their progeny. Does not the whole of the human race furnish a testimony to the mutual love and affection, attachment and devotion of Adam and his spouse? Verily, it is not at all difficult for God to bless the mates who are being united today in a holy wedlock to become one day the head of a large family, the progenitor of a happy and prosperous people.

"The sacred Scripture then asks you to remain conscious of God, in whose name you demand your rights from one another.

"The whole of human existence, the entire gamut of human activity is nothing more than a continuous demand made of one another. Whether it be government or business, education or industry, it is always a demand made by one man from the other; everyone asks the other for something and is in turn demanded to fulfil his own obligations. We are obliged to ask for one thing or the other from the lowest of the low in order to maintain social existence; for, every man has certain rights as well as obligations to others. This is, in reality, the sum and substance of a civilised social existence. And what is the inner content of this *nikah*, the nuptial tie? It is also a demand; nobly made and answered in a dignified way: a respectable family asks for the hand of the daughter of another equally worthy household to complete and consummate the life of its own son which had so long been imperfect and incomplete. They agree and unite the mates in the name of God. Now, two persons who had so long been complete strangers to one another, become a loving couple, admiring and adoring each other, as could be the supreme wish of any two mates. Their interests, their longings, their desires, nay, their destiny becomes one. This is all because of Allah, Holy is Whose name and Who turns that which is prohibited into permissible, tabooed into warranted, vice and sinfulness into virtue and righteousness and enables the couple to turn over a new leaf in their lives. It is on account of these Divine blessings that God enjoins you to be careful of your duty toward Him. There could be no act of greater ingratitude to Him than forgetting His name and your duties to Him after achieving your ends. You have to keep up His remembrance throughout your life, fulfil your duties unto Him in future and, as He has ordained, you have to be careful of the wombs that bare you, the ties of kinship that bind you.

"You are today entering into kinships that are entirely new to you. It would, therefore, be in the fitness of things to remind you of the old bonds of kinship which have by no means been weakened by the new one nor the duties and obligations owed unto them been rendered ineffectual. Therefore, you should never forget your duties to your mother in your zeal to fulfil your obligations as a husband nor forget your own father in your eagerness to please your father-in-law. Now some of you may think: who cares for these empty sermons and who can fulfil all these dual and onerous responsibilities? But God is All-Aware, All-Knowing! He reminds you that Allah hath been a Watcher over you. He alone is the Guardian, the Witness and the Watcher who shall ever be with you, and Who is nearer to you than your jugular vein.

"The next verse recited by me calls your attention to an unpalatable yet unavoidable fact. It is a prophet alone who has the courage to awaken the memory of an unpleasant thing like death on such a joyous occasion. But it is necessary that man should never forget, not for a moment, his ultimate end and guard the treasure which he would surely need in the After-life. This is the treasure of faith, the belief in God and unquestioning submission to His will. However prosperous, happy and long the life of a man may be, he has always to safeguard his faith and breathe his last in submission and servitude of the Lord and Master. This was in fact the key to the greatness of a man whom God had blessed with a wholesome countenance, wealth and power, glory and wisdom. Remember the Prayer offered when he was at the very top of worldly success one can aspire to. Said he: "*Oh my Lord! Thou hast given me (something) of sovereignty and hast taught me (something) of the interpretation of events – Creator of the heavens and the earth! Thou art my Protecting Friend in the World and the Hereafter. Make me to die submissive (unto thee), and join me to the righteous.*" (Yūsuf 12: 101).

> "Now, before you hear the bridegroom say, 'I consent,' for which you have all gathered here, you should listen to the Qur'an which says, '*Oh ye who believe, Guard your duty to Allah, and speak words straight to the point.*' It means that the bridegroom should only say that which is right, with full consciousness of the far-reaching consequences and the responsibilities devolving on him by his own words and that he should give his consent after realising the grave impact of this affirmation. The Qur'an then proceeds further to tell you that if somebody inculcates the habit of speaking with a sense of responsibility, he soon becomes trustworthy and reliable, truthful and righteous, his life becomes a beacon of light for others, a shining example, and worthy of redemption and the blessings of God. Finally, this solemn verse of the Qur'an emphasises that real success lies with God Alone: it depends on submission to the Master and His Messenger and not on following one's desires, nor on the performance of rites and customs."

The offer and acceptance of the *nikah* follows the *khutbah*, after which dates are distributed or showered. This also emulates the *Sunnah* (practice) of the Prophet which is still followed by the Muslims of India and elsewhere.

Misuse of *Mahr*

The *mahr* or dower-money paid by the husband to his wife is an essential feature of Muslim marriages, but the prevalent custom among Indian Muslims is peculiar to them and reflects the airiness of their manners. The more the amount of *mahr,* the more it is appreciated by the parties concerned and a surer guarantee of the stability and continuity of the marital tie. Sometimes the *mahr*, fixed according to this usage, is an imaginary figure which is, of course, never paid. Departing from the old convention, people now tend to have a more realistic *mahr*. The religious law of Islam does not fix any particular amount of *mahr* but leaves it to be determined in accordance with the social and economic position of the husband. Nevertheless, Islam favours a moderate *mahr* which should be paid outright before the marriage or at least promised to be paid later on, otherwise the *nikah* is void *ab initio*, reducing itself to a promiscuous relationship. This is obviously only possible in cases where the *mahr* is moderate enough that it can be paid by the husband.

Other Manners and Customs

After describing the customs relating to the marriage of Indian Muslims, it appears necessary to mention briefly certain other features of their social life.

Everybody falls ill at one time or another for no one is immune from it. Prayer five times a day or the *namaz*, as it is called, is an obligatory duty to be performed even during periods of illness. The *Shari'ah*, however, allows certain concessions to such persons. If he is unable to walk down to the mosque to offer his Prayer with the congregation, he can perform it alone at his home. Similarly, if he cannot stand up, he can offer it sitting or lying as may be convenient to him. He can even offer it up through gestures if he is too ill to perform it in any other manner. If he cannot use water for ablution, he may take resort to *tayammum*[7] but he has to be careful to follow the rules of purification.

Paying a visit to the sick and afflicted is a meritorious act in the eyes of Islam. One is, however, forbidden to remain longer with a sick person than is absolutely necessary unless the patient himself desires a prolonged sitting. The rules of etiquette prescribed by the traditions of the Holy Prophet (peace be upon him) require that one should always keep in view the inconvenience caused to the patient or his attendants by a longer sitting during such courtesy calls.

Death and Burial

Everybody born on this earth has to die one day. The inevitable last journey everybody has to undertake is attended everywhere with rituals prescribed by usage or the canons of religion. Indian Muslims have, likewise, their own customs and conventions some of which are prescribed by their religion, and others which have evolved or been borrowed from other people of the land.

The Last Wish

Every Muslim, high or low, pious or unorthodox, aspires to die with *kalimah-i-shahadat*, the article of Muslim affirmation, on his lips. This is because his greatest desire is to live and die with his faith intact in the Unity of God and the Prophethood of Muhammad (peace be upon him). In every Muslim society, provided it is permeated with religious teachings, even to the least extent, there is a standing convention that the people ask the learned and pious souls to pray that they should join the great majority in the state of *iman*. Such an invocation by a pious person is highly valued by every Muslim, no matter whether he is illiterate or a sinner for he sincerely desires to emulate a man who dies professing the name of God and affirming His Overlordship and praise.

As soon as the family perceives that the patient is close to death, all those present at the time exhort him to recite the *Kalimah*[8] or to keep himself busy in the remembrance of` God. However if he is too seriously ill to speak or even utter these words, the friends and relatives around him begin to recite the *Kalimah* or engage themselves in remembrance of God. If it is felt that the patient's throat is choked with thirst, water from the well of Zamzam,[9] or if that is not available, some fruit juice or sweet-drink is dropped into his mouth to provide relief from that agony. It is also recommended that the persons present at the time of someone's death should recite *Surah Yā Sīn* of the Qur'an. The face of the patient at the end of his life or when he has given up the soul is turned towards the *qiblah*.[10]

The Burial Ceremony

Soon after a Muslim dies, preparations start for the washing (*ghusl*) of his dead body and the provision of a shroud (*kafan*) for him. The shroud is always of a new white cotton cloth undefiled by any impurity and consists of a seamless shirt, a *tahband* or wrapping and a covering sheet. In the case of a woman, a head-cloth and a breast cover are the additional items of the shroud. The dead body is washed ceremoniously in the manner prescribed in the canon books. Although the dead body can be washed by any Muslim, it is considered preferable to entrust this task to those who are conversant with the rules of the *ghusl*. Near kin and friends of the deceased prefer to perform this last service to the departed soul themselves. However, in some places family barbers wash the corpse while in certain communities professional washers (*gassals*) are engaged to do this job.

After washing the dead body thoroughly with soap and water, dousing it over and over again with copious amounts of water, and drying it well, it is dressed in the shroud. Camphor is placed under each armpit and on the orifices of the body, and the arms are folded across his or her chest. Those who have already performed the *hajj* usually bring back their shrouds dipped in the water of Zamzam.

The Funeral Service

The dead body, washed and shrouded, is then brought out of the house. It is also customary to show the face of the deceased to relatives and neighbours before it is finally covered. Now, it is the time for the funeral service, which is an act of the highest merit not only for the deceased but also for all those participating in it. The number of participants in the funeral service, however, depends on the social status and contacts of the deceased, as well as on the religious sense of his neighbours. The funeral service or *namaz-i-janazah*, as it is known in India, is offered in congregation but unlike other Prayers, it has no genuflection and prostration. Worshippers stand in rows of odd numbers, three, five, seven, depending on the number of participants, with the right hand placed on the left below the navel, and are led by a pious or learned person who stands a few paces ahead of the front line. The corpse is placed in front of the *Imam* leading the Prayer, who begins it after obtaining the permission of the legal heir or the nearest kin present at the time. The funeral Prayer, recited silently has four *takbirs*[11] which intervene between the initial *du'a*[12] and *darud*[13] (recited with or without *Surah Fātiḥah*[14]) and the benediction for the invocation of Divine blessings on the soul of the dead person. This, being the chief supplication for the departed soul, is given here to acquaint readers with the type of Prayer made:

> "O Allah! Pardon our living and our dead, the present and the absent, the young and the old, the male and the female. O Allah! he (or she) to whom Thou accordest life, cause him to live on the (path of) Islam; and he to whom Thou givest death, cause him to die in (the state of) *iman*."

If, however, the deceased is a minor, then the *du'a* recited is as follows:

> "O Allah! Make him (or her) our forerunner and make him (or her), for us, a reward and a treasure, and make him (or her) for us a pleader, and accept his (or her) pleading."

After the fourth *takbir*, the Prayer is terminated with the *salaam*. The dead body is, thereafter, taken out to the burial place in a bier, or a cot, and carried by constantly changing relays of four men. The traditions of the Prophet (peace be upon him) recommend the accompaniment and carrying of the dead body as well as remaining in the cemetery until the dead body is buried as pious acts to be rewarded in the Hereafter. Every Muslim deems it his duty to carry the bier, whether the dead man was known to him or not and, as a consequence, there is never any difficulty in taking the dead body to the cemetery no matter how long a distance is to be covered or how unfavourable the weather is. Nowadays, in bigger cities the dead body is also taken on vehicular transport owing to the long distances to be covered. Although there is no harm in this, the better way of carrying the corpse and also in consonance with the practice followed by the Prophet (peace be upon him) is to carry it on the mourners' shoulders.

The Grave

The grave is got ready by the time the dead body reaches the cemetery. The corpse is then taken by hand and placed in it, the face of the deceased pointing towards the *qiblah*, and then the grave is closed with wooden planks and mud in such a way that earth will not enter therein. All those present at the time help in filling the grave with mud, with the following Qur'anic supplication on their lips:

> "*Thereof We created you, and there unto We return you, and thence We bring you forth a second time.*" (Ṭā Hā 20: 55).

Having covered the grave with mud in the shape of a rounded mound, everyone leaves the place but those who have been close to the deceased normally stay for a while reciting the Qur'an and praying for the redemption of the dead soul.

Rites Performed After Death

The family which suffers the bereavement is normally provided with food by relatives and friends for three days or three times. This is a custom sanctioned by the practice followed during the life-time of the Prophet (peace be upon him), since it is considered that the members of the deceased's family are too grief-stricken to make culinary arrangements themselves.

Prayers for the Departed Soul

Indian Muslims have adopted several rites relating to the Prayer for the dead and the funeral banquet, repeated on various dates after the death occurs, and which seem to have been derived from local custom as they are not found in any other Islamic country. Some of the special rites performed after death are called *tija*,[15] *chaliswan*[16] and *qul*[17] which are performed on certain specified dates with set customary rituals. There is also the custom of celebrating the *Urs*, resembling a fair held on the birth or death anniversary, normally on the latter occasion, of pious and holy persons. The name of the last-mentioned celebration is derived from the Arabic term for wedding, and has the connotation of the mystic union of the saint with God. Muslims of other countries are not conversant with such celebrations. On these occasions, the followers of the saint come to the grave of the saint, often from far-off places, for recitation of the Qur'an and the invocation of Divine blessings for their departed mentor. Public banquets known as *langar* are arranged on these occasions in which everyone, the poor and the rich, partake their meals. Muslims of some other countries too organise certain functions for the commemoration of the memory of their saints, the propagation of their teachings and the offering of supplications for them, but these differ from the customs followed by Indian Muslims. These are also not known by the name *Urs*.

NOTES

1. The Persians also had four major classes, namely priests, warriors, commoners and serfs, and this is almost identical to the Indian Varnas.
2. Both derive from the Arabic *sharif* meaning honourable.
3. For details *see* Qur'an: 4: 22–36.
4. A distinguished Companion of the Prophet (peace be upon him), 'Abdur Rahman ibn 'Auf, married after his migration to Madinah. The Prophet (peace be upon him) came to know of it the next day on account of the scent 'Abdur Rahman had used. The Prophet (peace be upon him) then asked him to invite his friends to a *valima* or feast. (Bukhari, Muslim).
5. Under Islamic Law, any major male member of the family in possession of sound mental faculties who is also a heir of the girl and allowed to give consent on her behalf is called a *wali*.
6. *Sunnah* the way of the Prophet (peace be upon him). *Sunnah* and *hadith* denote sayings, acts and ritual approval of the Prophet (peace be upon him).
7. A ritual method of purification for Prayer in place of *wudu'*, when water is not available or cannot be used.
8. *La ilaha illallah Muhammad ur-rasool ullah:* There is no god but Allah; Muhammad is the Messenger of Allah.
9. The well within the precincts of the mosque of the Ka'bah.
10. i.e. the Ka'bah.
11. The formula, meaning "Allah is Great."
12. Meaning "supplication."
13. Invocation of Divine blessings for the Prophet.
14. The first chapter of the Qur'an.
15. Consisting of the recitation of the Qur'an and supplication for the dead on the third day after the death.
16. Rites performed on the fortieth day, consisting of Prayer for the dead soul and a funeral banquet.
17. A death anniversary when supplications are made for the deceased.

III

SOCIAL CUSTOMS

An Admixture of Islamic and Indian Cultures

The social life of Indian Muslims, the pattern of their family life in particular, does not present any marked divergence from the surrounding culture of the people among whom they happen to reside. In a country so vast as India, with its varying climatic conditions, economic and social differences, the culture of the Indian Muslims too is marked by distinctive features, customs and manners like that of their local compatriots, in different parts of the country. This is a natural development, yet, the Indian Muslim culture in almost every part of the country, is also permeated to an extent with the spirit of Islam. The varying cultures of different regions have always been, and still are, enlivened by certain distinctive characteristics, ceremonies, rites and practices, which are common to all of them. These typical features also lend them a colour of their own within the local or regional social pattern. The origin of the common traits of Indian Muslim culture can be traced to the influences left by the Turko-Iranian culture, imported from Iran, Turkistan and Afghanistan and represented for quite a long period in India by the Turk, Afghan and Moghul rulers as well as the landed and military aristocracy of the time. Another streak of this culture is drawn from the post-Islam Arab culture which has always been valued by the Muslims as the ideal way of life. These two elements have blended with Indian customs and manners, rites and traditions to produce an entirely new and typical social pattern standing apart from all yet resembling in certain aspects each one of these. It is, in fact, a composite culture which is neither Islamic in its true sense, nor Iranian, Turkish or Indian. It can only be called the Indo-Islamic culture.

The *Purdah* System

Among well-to-do Muslims who also regard themselves as belonging to the higher strata or *ashraf* the *purdah* system is still observed to a great extent. Without entering into the controversy about whether it is Islamic or un-Islamic or how far it is necessary or practicable, it can be asserted that the *purdah* so punctiliously observed a few decades earlier, has now lost its rigour owing, chiefly, to modern education and economic and social changes overtaking the country. It has indeed been completely given up by certain "modernised" Muslim families. Muslim ladies who earlier moved out in covered planquins, *dolis* and *muhafas* or completely veiled coaches and victorias are now obliged to go about in tongas, rikshaws and buses leaving aside earlier scruples. Also, the spread of education among girls, especially in urban centres, has further curtailed the *purdah* system.

Even the *purdah* that used to be earlier observed in Muslim families could hardly be regarded as complying with the Islamic injunction, if only because the prevalent custom never required seclusion from certain relatives expressly directed to be kept aloof from the kindred women. The social custom adopted by Indian Muslims however, took what may be called a broader view in regard to these kinships, following their compatriots, although the practice often proved to be fraught with dangerous consequences.

Purdah Observed by Women

The *purdah* observed by the would-be bride from her female in-laws is a purely Indian custom. In certain families it is so rigidly followed that prospective brides begin to observe *purdah* from their own kin, such as aunts, from the time they are betrothed to their cousins. No such custom is, however, to be found among Muslims in other countries.

Hospitality and Generosity

In well-to-do Muslim families, particularly those which are socially well-connected, there are almost always a few guests. If such families reside in a city, they usually have a few relative students coming from rural or sub-urban areas for higher studies. Such families more often than not have several dependants sharing the earnings of one person. The abolition of *Zamindaris* and *jagirs* as well as the rising spiral of prices have seriously curtailed this practice but it is still in vogue among Muslims to an appreciable extent. The merits of hospitality and generosity to be shown to guests and the obligations of neighbourliness expounded in the teachings of Islam, the example set by the pious and religious precursors of the old and the Arab and Afghan traditions of gracious hospitality have assigned it a place of religious and moral duty in Muslim society. Muslims still consider it propitious to entertain and receive their guests with open arms. They also consider it a duty enjoined by religion to maintain cordial relations with their neighbours and present gifts to them on special occasions.[1]

Table Manners

All the members of a family generally take their meals together, unless there is some difficulty in this. In cities, nowadays, preoccupations of profession, educational needs and similar other difficulties do not allow all the members of a family to assemble for meals at the appointed time. Nevertheless, as far as possible all members of the family prefer the practice of dining together while, in certain families, men and women partake of their food jointly in separate shifts. Since the institution of untouchability is altogether alien to the tenets of Islam, the utensils used by one man while taking food or drinking water are freely used by the other. Not only are the bowls, saucers and tumblers used by one member not avoided by others, often two, or more persons partake of food from the same bowl or saucer or take whatever is left by the other. Now, modern Western table manners and medical culinary directives have begun to make inroads into the equalitarian and fraternal traditions of Muslim society.

The utensils in common use in Muslim houses are generally spacious and large. The edibles left over by guests at feasts are not thrown away but given to the servants or the poor and needy. In Arabia, however, there being absolutely no inhibition in this regard, the host and his family members eat any of the meal that is left by guests.

The Caste System among Indian Muslims

The social life of Indian Muslims shows a striking contrast between the Islamic belief in equality and universal brotherhood on the one hand, and the superstructure of social discrimination adopted by them on the other. The Muslims of India have, undoubtedly, developed a social hierarchy based on the birth of the individual but unlike the caste system of the Hindus, their's does not insist on complete social segregation or untouchability nor does it stand in the way of anyone achieving social eminence or the respect of society. However, those Indian Muslims who were gradually converted to Islam from the indigenous population retained some of their social customs including the caste structure and occupations, and, thus, introduced the counterpart castes of the Hindus into the social structure of Indian Islam.

The descendants of Muslim immigrants to the country, on the other hand, fitted into the then social structure by claiming the highest ranks by virtue of their being related to the ruling races such as the *Moghuls* and *Pathans*, or because they belonged to the lineage of early Muslim nobility as *Sayyeds* and *Shaikhs*. These sections being closer to the ruling elite of the Muslim era, naturally, came to regard themselves as *ashraf* or *shurafaa*, i.e. belonging to a higher rank than others. The *Sayyeds* claim their descent from the Prophet, while *Shaikhs* regard themselves as descendants of the nobility of early Islam. These two constitute the top-grade of the Muslim caste hierarchy, and the remaining, as their name indicates, are ethnic groups who take their place after the first two. It seems that converts from the high caste Hindus were gradually assimilated by one or the other *ashraf* castes as, for example, the *Rajput* converts to Islam generally use the appellation of *Khan* with their names and the *Kashmiri Brahmans* are all known as *Shaikhs*. Other sections of Indian Muslims, i.e. converts from the low ranking castes of Hindus, generally retained their caste occupations such as those of the *Dhobi* (laundryman), *Julaha* (weaver), *Gaddi* (grazer or milkman), *Nai* or *Hajjam* (barber), etc. Some of these appear to have converted *en masse*: *Gaddis, Julahas, Bhishtis* (water-carriers) and a few other castes are now entirely Muslim while others have their corresponding castes among the Hindus. However, it is difficult to maintain that all these castes among the Muslims are converts from the corresponding Hindu castes for some of them such as *Darzi* (tailors), *Qassab* (butchers), *Mirasi* (musicians) and a few similar castes seem to have derived their names from occupations taken up after their conversion to Islam. Some of the lower castes have strictly maintained their endogamous social circle or *biradri* system like their Hindu counterparts which prohibits, on the one hand, marriage outside those castes and also serves, on the other, as a social constraint for erring members overstepping caste taboos or other moral limits under the compulsion of excommunication from the *biradri.*

The disappearance of the feudal system which had kept most lower castes pegged to their occupations in rural areas, the recent trend of urbanisation with industrial expansion and the resultant changes in the socio-economic structure of society, have combined to accelerate the breaking-up of certain occupational castes no longer useful to society. Some of these castes, particularly those having smaller numbers or engaged in a defunct occupation, are gradually merging into other occupational units of equal rank by adopting new professions or by establishing matrimonial relations with other castes. Such castes include the *Bhatyaras, Daphalis,* etc.

Caste Attitudes

In general, Muslims belonging to the higher castes maintain an attitude of superiority as against the lower ranks. Among themselves, they enjoy free social intercourse, although with varying endogamic customs which differ from place to place and from family to family. Certain families giving undue importance to the purity of blood are far more strict in contracting marriages outside their own caste, or, for that matter, even outside their own family circle. Others among the *ashraf* ranks, however, take wives of the castes regarded next below to their own, but do not, as a rule, give their own daughters in marriage to them. It is of interest to mention here the Muslim view of *kufw* which also has the sanction of religious canons. Muslim legists recognise the necessity of the social-equality of matches for a happy and successful marriage but this has nothing to do with racial superiority or social discrimination as sometimes exhibited by higher rank Indian Muslims. The concept of *kufw* only purports to ensure that the husband should not come from such a lower social stratum that the wife or her relations should feel disgraced by the marriage. The rule places no restraint on marriages between couples belonging even to two different races if they are otherwise socially, economically and culturally equal.

The air of superiority exhibited by the *ashraf* classes has been limited, for all practical purposes, to the rule of endogamy and a few other social customs without any appreciable affect on the free social intercourse between the lower and the higher castes of Indian Muslims. An interesting feature of the custom followed in this regard is the exclusion of lower caste Muslims from the ceremonial feasts of higher caste Muslims. The former, if invited, are not allowed to partake their meals with the latter; likewise, servants in Muslim households of position and rank are made to take their meals separately after other members of the family or relatives belonging to the higher castes have taken their food.[2] On the other hand, persons belonging to the higher castes, however poor or whatever occupation they may be engaged in, can claim equality of status in such social functions with their well-to-do relatives. These customs are to a large extent the product of a feudal system under which the higher castes were generally landowners and the lower castes tillers of the soil or engaged in occupations of a lower social order. Despite these customs, however, there has never been any social segregation or untouchability and higher caste Muslims freely take food with lower castes on informal occasions or when invited to the social functions of lower caste Muslims.

Attitude with Regard to Callings and Professions

As already stated, most lower castes of Indian Muslims have been associated and identified with the specific trades or callings in which they have been engaged but there has never been any restriction on changing one's occupation. An occupation generally regarded as belonging to a lower caste, as, for example, the profession of a *Darzi* (tailor) or a *Dhobi* (laundryman) is often adopted by a person belonging to a higher caste without any effect on his caste status. In fact, Muslims have never accepted occupations as permanent and unchangeable professions of particular castes, nor does the division of labour depend on "caste" in the form of social classes, as recognised by Indo-Iranian people. Nor has the caste system among Indian Muslims ever discouraged people belonging to a lower social unit or engaged in any one of the lower caste trades or callings to adopt a respectable profession like the teaching of religious sciences or acting as *Imams* and preachers (*khatibs*). In fact, Islam does not look down upon any lawful profession with disrespect. In other predominantly Muslim countries, particularly in Arab lands, Makkah and Madinah, several respected doctors of religion have surnames[3] indicating the occupation of their forefathers. These occupational surnames are neither held in contempt by anybody nor do the persons using them feel shame because of those appellations.

There is no denying the fact that Indian Muslims have gradually absorbed numerous traits from their Hindu neighbours including their caste system but the rigour of social discrimination implied in the system was softened to a large extent by the egalitarian principles of Islam. The reason for this apparent complexity in the social attitude of Indian Muslims can be traced to the segregating influence of the institution of the Indian caste system and the air of superiority produced by the feudal system on the one hand, and on the other the uncompromising teachings of Islam declaring that the whole of mankind is the progeny of Adam,[4] that honour in the sight of God depends on piety – God-consciousness[5] and that no Arab has a preference over a non-Arab nor a non-Arab over an Arab.[6]

The Dress of Indian Muslims

The gradual process of the Indianisation of Muslims did not manifest itself only in the assimilation of the cultural and social traits of their neighbours and its flowering in new forms of social relationships, but it also evolved new raiments and costumes in unison with their taste and suitability to local climatic conditions. By and large, their dress is the legacy of the Indo-Islamic culture which was developed and refined by the end of Moghal rule in India and reached its apex in the cultural centres of Delhi, Lucknow and Hyderabad where the Hindu nobility also adopted Muslim dress. There is no appreciable difference in the dress of the Muslim nobility whether living in the northern regions or in the southern states of the country, nor does the dress of Muslims of the upper and middle classes show any marked variation. It consists of trousers of different shapes like *pyjamas, shalwars* and *ghararas* with a shirt (including *kurta*) and a long coat called *sherwani*, which is an improved form of the *achkans* and *angarkhas* worn earlier. The caps worn are of different shapes. Those more prevalent in Oudh and Bihar are *do-pallis*. Other popular head-dresses among Muslims include a cap made of velvet and known as a Rampuri cap, and a boat-shaped cap called the Gandhi or Ajmal cap. The latter is commonly worn by Hindus too. Turbans or *pagrees* are now falling into disuse even among the *'Ulama'* (religious teachers) but these can still be seen at certain places worn by bridegrooms during marriage ceremonies. *Lungi* is also commonly worn in certain places for the convenience of working at home or in the fields, but its size and shape as well as the way it is put on differs from the *dhoti* generally worn by Hindus. In certain rural areas, however, the *dhoti* is the common dress of the Hindus as well as of the Muslims.

Muslim Dwellings

The increasing impact of the Western mode of living as well as the emphasis on town planning in recent years is tending to obliterate the differences in the design of Muslim dwellings and the style of houses built by other communities. The houses now built with the approval of town planning and municipal authorities are, by and large, of the same type meant for renting out to tenants who abound in cities. However, the residential structures built earlier by the Muslims were almost always well ventilated and spacious with a wide courtyard but where the inside view was secluded from the outside. Two other features of houses were that the lavatories were always constructed in a way that one did not have to face the *qiblah* while excreting or urinating. Muslims are forbidden to sit facing the Ka'bah while answering the call of nature and, hence, this precaution had to be taken in every Muslim country in the construction of their houses. Indian Muslim houses also had bathrooms secluded from public view and had a raised platform on which to keep the buckets in order to comply with the rules of ritual purification.

The Decoration of Houses

If you enter the house of an average Indian Muslim, you will invariably find copies of the Holy Qur'an in different sizes kept in a niche wrapped in cloth coverings. In certain families every member, young or old, daily recites the sacred Scripture early in the morning. The decoration of houses with pictures of animate objects having been prohibited by Islam, wall-texts bearing Qur'anic verses or a few lines by some well-known poet written in a flowery pattern can be seen adorning the walls in almost every middle-class house. In certain modernised households, nowadays, who have shaken off the grip of religion, pictures have found a place as decorative pieces.

Arrangements for Offering Prayers

In almost every house one will find prayer-mats or a sheet of cloth set apart for offering Prayers. Women, who are normally more religious-minded everywhere, perform the Prayers regularly in the privacy of their homes. Male members of the family usually perform their Prayers in the mosque but some of them have to offer it up in the house owing to illness or some other inability. For such occasions, as well as for guests who might prefer to perform the service alone, a small wooden prayer-bench is also available in every house along with the prayer-mat. Everyone in the house, young or old, is fully aware of the direction of the *qiblah* and also abides by the precautionary measures meant for showing due deference to the Ka'bah. In certain sophisticated families a separate *lota* or jug is set apart for performing ablutions. It would not be out of place to mention here that the *lota*[7] or jug with a beak-shaped pipe attached to it has been in common usage among Muslims for a long time. It ensures economical use of water and, being of a slightly larger size, is very convenient for performing ablutions.

The Position of Women in Muslim Society

The position of women in Muslim society has always been a far more respected and happier one than that of their sisters elsewhere.

Upon her falls the duty of managing the household, of cooking and purchasing provisions; she holds the honour and good name of her husband in the hollow of her hand and enjoys many legal rights conferred on her by the *Shari'ah* or religious law of Islam. As mistress of the house, she also has to look after the upbringing of the children and their education and manners. In most well-to-do houses, normally an old lady is engaged for religious education, especially for the teaching of the Qur'an, to children of a tender age. Children from neighbouring houses are also encouraged to receive free education from such tutors. In certain places, educated middle-class housewives teach the Qur'an to their neighbours' daughters without charging any fee for this. These informal schools are also a means of imparting training in sewing, embroidery and cooking.

Respect for the Elderly

Old age among Muslims is not something to be despised or denigrated. On the contrary, it demands the highest esteem and reverence, as a mark of respect for maturity in wisdom, and entitles one to greater love and care by younger members of the family. Anybody visiting a Muslim house will not unoften come across an old man and he may be a distant relative or the *Imam* of the local mosque, sitting on a prayer-mat engaged in the recollection of God. He will see members of the family making obeisance to him, saluting him in the morning and desirous of his blessings. No servant or child or an elder member of the family will show disrespect to him. Everybody deems it an honour to serve him, bring him food and do whatever he is bidden.

The same regard is paid if there is an old lady in the family. These ladies usually pass their time in Prayers and recollection of God, invoking Divine blessings for the women and children of the family and also neighbours, all of whom regularly pay a visit to them for that purpose. The blessings by such old ladies are considered efficacious for warding off evil. Whether such a lady is a blood relation or not, she is affectionately called grandma or aunty.

The Re-marriage of Widows

The re-marriage of widows is neither looked down upon by Islam nor has it ever been held in contempt by any custom or usage of Muslim peoples. The Prophet of Islam (peace be upon him) himself contracted marriages with widows and so did the pious and learned doctors of faith, kings and grandees in bygone ages. There being no inhibition whatsoever in this regard the widows of respectable and noble families were given in marriage for the second time by their own guardians, fathers and brothers. Several such examples of Moghul princes can be cited who were re-married after widowhood and who continued to receive the same respect by kings and relatives as well as by the then society. It seems (as related by Khafi Khan) that during the reign of Muhammad Shah (1719–48) the then nobility began to treat the re-marriage of widows with contemptuous disrespect. They began to view the second marriage as an affront to the family honour and as an act against the fidelity of the widows towards their late husbands. Anyone who dared to permit his widowed sister or daughter to re-marry was not only sneered at but had also to face the social boycott of his friends and relatives. The re-married widow and her husband sometimes even had to migrate from the place. This custom had so deeply rooted itself in Indian Muslim society that Sayyed Ahmad Shahid Barelwi, the renowned reformer and religious leader of the nineteenth century, had to launch a movement against it; he and his followers fought this innovation relentlessly. For this purpose, they even had to set personal examples before the practice of re-marrying widows was revived. It was owing to his indefatigable efforts that widow re-marriage is no longer held in contempt among Indian Muslims as it was a century or two earlier. Although some widows still do not re-marry for various reasons quite a large percentage of them are now re-married.

Muslim Greetings

Among Muslims all over the world the customary greeting, as also required by their religion too, is *assalam-o-'alaikum* (peace be upon you) with the reply *wa 'alaikum-us-salam* (on you too be peace). In certain towns, particularly those of Oudh, one is greeted by *adab'arz* (I pay my respects to you). This is also accompanied by younger people bowing down before their elders as a mark of respect for them. In places like Hyderabad, this particular way of salutation is repeated three or four times. This over-sophisticated way of salutation, known as *farshi salaam*, is replied by *tasleem*, or an expression of the wish to live long. These greetings are also followed by a handshake sometimes with both hands. On the occasion of *'Id* or when a close friend or relation returns from a journey the congratulatory greeting is normally a prelude to a warm embrace.

Remembrance of God

Throughout his life the name of God is constantly on the lips of a Muslim, whether learned or illiterate, young or old. Words and phrases praising God have so become part and parcel of his daily conversation that one is constantly reminded of the Omnipotence, Overlordship, Bounty and Munificence of God Almighty at every turn. Some of these recurrent phrases commonly repeated on different occasions are:

> *Alhamdu lillah* (Praise be to God) to express gratitude or return thanks for kindness.

Masha' Allah (with the Will and Mercy of God) on the occasion of happiness or to congratulate others.

Insha' Allah (except if Allah Wills) while making a promise or expressing the intention to do something in future.

Inna lillahi wa inna ilaih-i-rajï'oon (we all belong to Allah and unto Him shall we return) to express resignation when one has sustained a loss.

La haula Wala Quwwata illa billah (there is no might nor majesty except in God) to express resentment or indignation.

Subhan Allah (Glory be to God) to express astonishment at some strange sight.

Bismillah (in the name of God) is said before one begins to take food, and then finishes it with *Alhamdu lillah*. Similarly, in order to excuse oneself from accepting an invitation one says: *Barak Allah* (may God bless you).

Anybody who sneezes says: *Alhamdu lillah* (Praise be to God) and gets the reply: *Yarhamuka Allah* (may God have mercy on you). He then has to return the invocation by the phrase: *Yahdikumullah wa yusleh balakum* (May God guide you on the right path and help you).

Rules of Common Courtesy

Whenever someone pays a visit to a middle-class Muslim household he is usually felicitated with betel-leaves. The offering of a betel to guests is an old Indian custom which was adopted by Indian Muslims as early as the fourteenth century. The custom, prevalent in the monasteries of Muslim saints and Sufi's, finds mention in the records of their discourses and biographies. Although the custom of offering betels to guests is followed almost all over India, it is more widespread in Uttar Pradesh, Bihar and Deccan. Oudh, in Uttar Pradesh, being more sophisticated has developed different ways of preparing the betel-leaves, as, for instance, their flowery display in a saucer, before these are presented to guests. Small betel-boxes with fine metalwork on them and cloth pouches with exquisite embroidery demonstrate the interest as well as the refined tastes of the people. Tobacco is also taken with betels. It is prepared in numerous ways to give it varying flavours, tastes and agreeable fragrances. Lucknow is the centre for manufacturing betel and chewing tobacco, known also as *zarda* and *surti*, which is relished all over the country. The old habit of smoking waterpipes or *hukka* is giving way to the more convenient smoking of cigarettes and cigars. However, people can still be seen enjoying the luxury of smoking the *hukka* which was once the symbol of the old culture and an inalienable part of all social gatherings.

'Atar and Perfumes

Indian Muslims have always had a taste for perfumes and this is also encouraged by the rules of the *Shari'ah* and the practice of the Holy Prophet (peace be upon him).[8] The development of the perfume industry owes much to the efforts of Indian Muslims who invented numerous varieties of *'atar* which are renowned the world over.

NOTES

1. The rights of neighbours as enjoined by the teachings of Islam admit of no distinction between Muslim and non-Muslim. During the time of the Prophet (peace be upon him), his Companions used to treat their Jewish neighbours kindly despite their uncooperative behaviour towards them, and sent gifts to them regularly.
2. In other Muslim countries, particularly Arabia and Afghanistan, household servants usually take their food with the members of the family.

3. For instance, the *khatib* and *Imam* of the *Haram* (Mosque of the Ka'bah) has *khayyat*, i.e. a tailor as his surname. Similarly, there are other learned *'Ulama'* (religious scholars) who use the appellations of *hallaq* (barber), *zayyat* (*teli* or oil-presser), *Sawwaf* (seller of cotton), or *Qassab* (butcher) and these surnames are not looked down upon by anybody.
4. An-Nisā' 4: 1.
5. Al-Ḥujurāt 49: 13.
6. *Musnad* of Imam Ahmad ibn Hanbal.
7. Perhaps the remark of Jawahar Lal Nehru in his autobiography that he did not find any difference between the Hindu and Muslim cultures excepting the special design of the Muslim *lota*, has given it an ignominious publicity.
8. The Holy Prophet (peace be upon him) had a liking for '*atar* and other perfumes with which he scented his clothes on each Friday and on the occasion of *'Id*. It is related that the *atar* used by him on the occasion of his last *hajj* was imported from India.

IV

FEASTS AND FESTIVALS

The *'Id* Festivals

The two great festivals of the Muslim world are *'Id-ul-Fitr* and *'Id-ul-Adha*, commonly known in India as *'Id* and *Baqra'id*. The *'Id* falls immediately after the close of *Ramadan* or the month of fasting, that is, on the first of *Shawwal*, the tenth month of the Islamic calendar. *Ramadan* is spent in fasting and Prayer, self-denial and restraint and spiritual and moral discipline, for a full lunar month, and, therefore the arrival of *'Id* is eagerly awaited by followers of the Prophet's faith (peace be upon him). Naturally, the sighting of the new moon on the twenty-ninth day of *Ramadan* provides an occasion for such additional joy that the new moon on *'Id* and the crescent of the twenty-ninth day have become proverbial for great joyfulness. Every Muslim, rich or poor, young or old, has his gaze fixed on the sky to spot the silvery bow of the twenty-ninth of *Ramadan*. If it is not sighted on that evening, the day following is again spent in fasting. The crescent moon on the thirtieth day is, however, a certainty. As soon as a Muslim sights the new moon of *'Id*, he congratulates everybody around him; happiness is in the air, and all is pleasure and excitement. The young vie with each other to break the news first to their elders and receive their blessings. Those who have spent one whole month in the exhausting but pleasurable penance Pray thus to God on sighting the moon:

> "(O Moon) My Lord and thy Lord is one. Thou art the moon of guidance and betterment (for me). O Allah! Let this month begin for me with peace and (intact) faith and submission to Thy Will and Pleasure and with (my) ability to follow Thy Commandments."

For weeks beforehand people have been making preparations for the *'Id* but the night preceding it everybody is unusually busy in getting ready his new clothes and making sundry arrangements for the great occasion. The morning of the festival witnesses hectic preparations for the *'Id* Prayer. As a token of Divine permission to take food during the daytime after a month, sweets or dates are taken early in the morning. Everyone then takes a bath and puts on new clothes if he has the means. Perfumes are also used provided one can afford them, before setting out for Prayers in the *'Idgah*. All such persons as are liable to offer the charity enjoined for the occasion and known as *sadqa-i-Fitr* (charity of *'Id*), must pay it to the poor in the shape of grains or in cash before leaving for Prayers. This is a thanksgiving for having completed the fast of *Ramadan*. The measures prescribed by the *Shari'ah* for this offering is 1.63 kilograms of wheat or double its weight if it be barley. An amount equivalent to the market price of these grains can also be given in cash to the poor and needy. The measure fixed is for each individual and, therefore, it must be paid on behalf of all dependants, including minor children.

Now, the Prayer of *'Id* can be performed. It is better to offer this thanksgiving Prayer as early as possible but, again, the practice of the Holy Prophet (peace be upon him) has to be followed in its celebration. Thus, in emulation of the Prophet of Islam (peace be upon him) the *'Id* Prayer is offered after sunrise. But the time taken in making preparations on this occasion has again to be taken into consideration which means a bit more delay. Nevertheless, the Prayer is offered in India not later than ten or eleven in the morning. It is always preferable to offer this Prayer in the *'Idgah*, normally located in an open space outside the town. But increasing distances, rises in population and paucity of time have given rise to the custom of offering the Prayer in different localities of the city. Still, the congregation in the *'Idgah* is almost everywhere the largest in the city.

The *'Id* Prayer

When Muslims take the road for *'Idgah* they chant, in low tones, their praise and thanks of God. The practice of the Prophet (peace be upon him), still to some extent followed by Muslims, was to take one route for the *'Idgah* and return by another one so that all the pathways and sidewalks were filled with the adoration and glorification of the Lord and the devotion of the worshippers.[1] As cities have grown much larger and transport is easily available, the practice of taking different routes for going and returning is gradually being given up.

Contrary to the daily and Friday Prayers, the *namaz* of *'Id* is neither preceded by the *Adhan* nor by the *iqamah* or any obligatory or voluntary Prayer. As soon as the congregation is ready or the time for Prayer arrives, the *Imam* steps forward to lead the *namaz*. It has six extra *takbirs*, three in each *rak'at*, according to Hanafi *sunnis* who form the majority of Muslims in India. The *Imam* ascends the pulpit soon after the Prayer comes to an end with the final salutation, and delivers the sermon of *'Id* like the preachment of Fridays; it is also divided into two parts, which are separated by a brief respite by the sermoner. The sermon of *'Id*, however, differs from that of the Friday one inasmuch as the former is delivered after the Prayer while the latter is read before the *namaz*. In India, the address is normally read out in Arabic from some book but now at least one of the two parts are delivered in Urdu or any other regional language. This practice is being adopted to let the audience know the importance of the occasion, its liturgical rules and the demands of faith and its relevance to modern times.

Customary Greetings after the Prayers

As soon as the sermon ends, people begin congratulating and embracing each other. Indian Muslims alone take resort to embracing as a sign of affection on the occasion of *'Id*; the Muslims of other countries simply exchange greetings or shake hands. The practice does not have the sanction of the *Shari'ah* either, nor of any previous tradition; it seems to have been adopted by the Muslims of India from the prevalent custom of embracing on the occasion of Hindu festivals, particularly *Holi Milan*, which is considered to be an occasion of gaiety and merriment, festivity and fraternity in India.

On return from *'Idgah*, it is customary to pay a visit to friends and kin where one is entertained with sweetened vermicelli. Unlike other countries where guests are entertained with other sweetmeats and are sprinkled with *'atar* or any other perfume, vermicelli has become an inevitable must and a symbol of *'Id-ul-Fitr* in India.

'Id-ul-Adha

'Id-ul-Adha or *Baqra'id* differs from *'Id-ul-Fitr* inasmuch as a sacrifice is also offered up on this occasion. It is celebrated on the tenth day of *Dhil Hijjah*, the last month of the Islamic calendar, when, after performing the rites of *Hajj*, the Makkan pilgrims

gather at Mina at a distance of four miles from the Holy city for offering sacrifice and worship and recollection of God. Like *'Id-ul-Fitr*, the *'Id* Prayer on this occasion too is recited on the first day of the festival but sacrifice can be offered till the evening of the third day following it. For four days on this occasion, i.e. from the morning of the ninth to the afternoon (*'asr*-Prayer) of the thirteenth *Dhil Hijjah*, praise and glory of God is recited after every Prayer. Known as *takbirat-i-tashriq*, the purport of the words recited is as follows:

> "Allah is Most Great! Allah is Most Great!
> None is worthy of being worshipped except Allah!
> Allah is Most Great!
> Allah is Most Great and All Praise is for Allah alone."

The sacrifice offered on the day of *'Id-ul-Adha* has been instituted in commemoration of Abraham's willingness to offer up his only son, Ismael, as a sacrifice. The sacrificial offering is divided into three portions, one being set apart for household consumption, another for friends and relatives and the third for the poor and needy. The distribution of the offering, enjoined by the *Shari'ah*, is designed to provide a healthy and hearty meal to the poor on this festive occasion. No fasting is allowed on the day of *'Id-ul-Fitr* nor on the three sacrificial days of *'Id-ul-Adha*.

International Festivals

'Id-ul-Fitr and *'Id-ul-Adha* are the two principal festivals of the Muslim world. There being no dispute about the religious sanctity of the two festivals, these are observed without any exception, in every country where Muslims reside, raising them to the level of international festive occasions. There is also no marked difference in the manner in which these are celebrated in different countries: the religious rites performed on both these

days have been too well defined by the Qur'an and the *Sunnah* of the Holy Prophet (peace be upon him) to allow any variation in their observance in any country, whether Muslims are in a minority there or if they form a majority.

Other Festivals

Now to mention briefly a few other festivals, some of which are of local importance or are observed in India alone. The usages and customs forming part of a few of these are either unknown to the Muslim world or differ from the traditional form of their observance prevalent in India.

The Prophet's Birthday (peace be upon him)

The festival of the Prophet's Birthday (peace be upon him) is celebrated on the 12th of *Rabi'-ul Awwal*,[2] the third month of the Muslim lunar year. Of all the festive days, excepting the two *'Id*s, the Prophet's Birthday is the most important and widely celebrated festival throughout the world of Islam. The occasion is marked by mammoth gatherings in which orations are delivered on the life and teachings of the Holy Prophet (peace be upon him).

In countries like India and Egypt, the main emphasis of these lectures is the birth of the Prophet (peace be upon him), from which it derives its commonly known name, *milad* or *maulood*. The custom attending the haranguing of the chief event differs from country to country; in certain places a salutation in honour of the Prophet (peace be upon him) is sung after describing his birth when everyone present in the *milad* is expected to stand erect as a mark of respect to the Messenger of God (peace be upon him). This is known as *qiyam*.[3] Elaborate arrangements for the lighting and decoration of the place of assembly with buntings and flags are usually made while sweetmeats are distributed at certain places after the meeting is over. Huge amounts are wasted on these elegant decorations in India which could otherwise be utilised for more useful purposes beneficial to the community and the country at large. Many educated persons as well as religious and social organisations designed to reform social evils are, however, trying to make these meetings more effective and simple in order to acquaint the masses with the life, teachings and achievements of the Prophet of Islam (peace be upon him). Another custom of recent origin and limited to a few large cities in India is to take part in processions on this occasion. Nowadays poetical symposia or *mushairas* have become an inevitable part of the public *milads* which sometimes continue for the whole night.

Muharram

Muharram is the first month of the Muslim lunar year. Before Islam, and after its advent too, *Muharram* has been regarded as a sacred month entitled to veneration of the faithful. Many important events occurred on the 10th of this month. One of these was the deliverance of Moses and the Israelites from the tyranny of Pharaoh. Moses and his followers had crossed over to Sinai from Egypt on that day and Pharaoh was drowned in the Red Sea along with his legions. It is related that a few months after his immigration to Madinah, the Prophet (peace be upon him) observed the Jews keeping fast[4] on the tenth of *Muharram*. The Prophet (peace be upon him) enquired why they did so. On being informed that it was a memorial of the deliverance of Moses and the children of Israel from the hands of Pharaoh, the Prophet (peace be upon him) said: "We have a greater right in Moses than they." So he fasted and commanded his followers to fast also. Thus, the fast on that day came to be regarded as obligatory before it was made optional with the advent of the *Ramadan* fast. Even now many Muslims given to religious observance among the Sunnis keep the fast on the 10th of *Muharram*.

A Sorrowful Day

This consecrated and propitious day was, however, to witness a shameful and accursed event which has turned it into a day of mourning for Muslims. This was the martyrdom of Husain, the second son of Fatimah, the Prophet's daughter. Husain refused to take the oath of fealty to the then Caliph Yazid and left Madinah for Kufa with a retinue of his women and children and close relatives. As he approached the plains of Karbala he was intercepted by a much larger and well-equipped army of the Caliph under the command of 'Ubaidullah ibn Ziyad, the Governor of Kufa. On the morning of the fatal day (*'ashura'*), the 10th of *Muharram*, 60 A.H. (22nd October, 679 A.D.), Husain fought bravely till the battle came to an end with the death of the last of his companions. The tragic death of Husain still awakens the sympathy of the faithful who commemorate the memory of his martyrdom with sorrow and indignation. The Shi'ahs of India take part in processions with *taziahs*[5] and *'alams*[6] on this occasion and have special gatherings to mourn the death of Husain. Their mourning lasts till the fortieth day of Husain's martyrdom, known as *chehalum*, which falls on the 20th of the succeeding month of *Safar*.

The *Muharram* celebrations by the Shi'ahs of Iraq and Iran, where they have sizeable populations, and in Oudh, especially Lucknow, where they ruled for 136 years, are quite impressive and marked by pomp and pageantry. Customs differ from place to place but they normally consist of a passion performance in the course of which more devout Shi'ahs beat their bodies and faces until blood flows, there are processions with *taziah*s and *tabut*s and assemblages are held to lament the martyrdom of Husain. These customs have undergone some changes during the course of time or have been reformed to an extent in certain places, but a greater part of the Shi'ah community still celebrates the function in the traditional manner.

Sunni Muslims normally do not participate in the passion performances and other celebrations of the Shi'ahs since they hold a slightly different view of this sorrowful incident from that of the Shi'ahs. The Sunnis too, look up to the martyrdom of Husain as an ennobling example of indomitable courage and valour, of willingness to lay down one's life for truth and justice and hold him to be a victim of tyranny and injustice but, in their view, it is not proper to give vent to one's feeling of sorrow through wailings and lamentations. They consider it un-Islamic to bemoan and cry over a past happening and fruitless too for those whose memory these celebrations seek to preserve. In their view, a more befitting way of commemorating the martyrdom of Husain is to inculcate the qualities he possessed and to stick to the path of righteousness like him in face of all odds and difficulties. Sunni Muslims, therefore, by and large, disassociate themselves from *Muharram* processions and other rites, preferring to offer solemn invocation of Divine blessings on Husain and his companions through special Prayers and recitation of the Qur'an. However, in certain places, especially in rural areas, the Sunnis too keep the *taziah*s and follow some of their own customary rites to celebrate *Muharram*.

Shab-i-Barat

Shab-i-Barat is another festival occupying an important place in Muslim social life. It falls on the night of the fifteenth of *Sha'ban*, the eighth month of the Muslim year. It is believed that God annually ordains on that night all the actions of mankind which they are to perform during the coming year, how long they shall live and when they shall die, what they shall earn or lose and the vicissitudes of fortune that shall befall them. It is therefore enjoined that the night should be spent in Prayer and recollection of God. Many persons also keep fast on the fourteenth of *Sha'ban* which is warranted as a commendable act of worship. During the night, people keep vigil, recite the Qur'an, offer benedictions for their own self and their near kin, and visit the cemetery to pray for dead relatives. Women, although forbidden to visit the cemetery, also accompany men to the burial ground. Another custom prevalent in India is to prepare *halwa*[7] on the occasion of *Shab-i-Barat.*

The un-Islamic Custom of *Shab-i-Barat*

Indian Muslims have somehow adopted the custom of enjoying fireworks on the night of *Shab-i-Barat.* The display of fireworks, costing quite a large sum of money, is something of the equivalent to the British Guy Fawke's night for Indian Muslims. There being no trace of this curious custom in any other Muslim country, it seems to have been taken over by Indian Muslims from the *Diwali* (*Dipavali*) festival of the Hindus.

Alvadā'

Alvadā' or *Jumu'at-ul-Wada'* is the last Friday of *Ramadan* which has assumed the importance of a festive day in India. It is considered propitious to offer the congregational Friday Prayer on the day of *Alvadā'* in the principal Mosque of the city. People from rural and sub-urban areas especially make a point of visiting the nearest city for this purpose. The Jamu' Masjid of Delhi has one of the largest congregations on this occasion when the gathering is almost as large as for the *'Id* Prayer. No trace of any such custom is to be found in early Islam. Nor is it mentioned in the traditions of the Prophet (peace be upon him) nor in the writings of early Muslim legists.

Some Other Festivals

The Twenty-seventh of the month of *Rajab* is commonly regarded as the day on which the Prophet (peace be upon him) made his celestial journey to Heaven. It relates to the Prophet's heavenly journey in which he was carried by Archangel Gabriel by night upon a heavenly steed from Makkah to the Mosque of Jerusalem, whence he was brought up through the seven heavens into the very presence of God. The traditions fixing the night of the twenty-seventh of *Rajab* for the celestial journey are, however, not regarded as authentic. The Shi'ahs also celebrate the anniversary of the birth of Caliph 'Ali on this day.

Another feast day celebrated enthusiastically is *Gayarahwin Sharif* when special prayers are held for the great mystic saint, Shaikh 'Abdul Qādir Jīlānī. Feasts are also held by certain people on this occasion.[8]

Muslim Festivals of Indian Origin

Apart from the festivals sanctioned by religious dogma or those celebrated in one form or another by the Muslims of other countries, there are certain other festive days of purely Indian origin. One of these is *rajbi* when sweetened bread is cooked and kept in an earthen pot as an offering to certain saints.[9] There are also fairs held on the first Thursday of each lunar month on the graves of certain saints, the annual *Urs* of Ghazi Mian held at Bahraich and similar other *melas* and fairs held every year to celebrate the death anniversary of numerous saints and holy men. The most important and the largest fair of this type is held at Ajmer in Rajasthan from the first to the sixth of *Rajab* every year to celebrate the *Urs* of a mystic saint, Shaikh Moinuddin Chishti Ajmeri. The fair is attended by people from far-off places within the country as well as pilgrims from abroad. However, orthodox Muslims who demand a religious sanction and a precedent from the practice followed by the precursors of Islam for every observance associated with religion, do not approve of these fairs and festivals. Nevertheless, most of the customs of Indian Muslims including those tending to observe these fairs and festivals with an air of gaiety and colourfulness bespeak of the impact of the rituals and customs followed by their compatriots on similar occasions.

NOTES

1. The practice also served to distribute the traffic on different routes.
2. Also known as *Bara Wafat,* it is commonly held that the Prophet (peace be upon him) was born and died on the same day.
3. Certain Muslims who follow the traditions of the Prophet (peace be upon him) meticulously and reject every custom unless backed by a confirmed practice of the Prophet (peace be upon him), do not stand up in the *Milads.* Their plea is that since the Prophet (peace be upon him) disliked the practice of standing up in his honour during his life-time, the practice in his absence is all the more reprehensible.
4. Fast of the "Day of Atonement" on the tenth of *Tishri,* the seventh month of the Jewish Calendar.
5. Models of the tombs at Karbala.
6. Flags, as if of Husain's party.
7. A sweetmeat made of sugar and flour. It is difficult to say how this custom came into vogue but a legend ascribes its origin to a saint of the first century A.H., Owais Qarni, who is known for his ardent love of the Prophet Muhammad (peace be upon him). Although a contemporary of the Prophet (peace be upon him), he did not meet him. It is related that when he heard that a few of the Prophet's teeth had been knocked out in the Battle of Uhud, he pulled out all of his own teeth. Members of his household had, therefore, to prepare *halwa* for him. There is, however, hardly any credence to this story.
8. The practice is not commended by Muslims belonging to the Deoband school of thought and those who more strictly follow the precepts of religion.
9. The custom started some six or seven decades ago. There are still certain persons alive who can tell how this festival originated and was adopted by the people.

V

THE CREED AND RELIGIOUS OBSERVANCES

The Unity[1] of Godhead

The eternal Message of Islam is based on three fundamentals: belief in the One and Only God, Prophethood and resurrection on the Day of Judgement.

Belief in One God as the sole and unassisted Author of all creation is the dominant teaching of Islam. Allah is the Creator of all things, and He is Guardian over all things. His are the treasures and the keys of the heavens and the earth. (Az-Zumar 39: 62–3). There is no God save Him, the ever-living, the self-subsistent fount of all being. Neither slumber overtakes Him, nor sleep. His is all that is in the heavens and all that is on earth. Who is there that could intercede with Him, unless it be by His leave? He knows all that lies open before men and all that is hidden from them, whereas they cannot attain to anything of His Knowledge save that which He wills them to attain. His eternal Glory overspreads the heavens and the earth, and their upholding wearies Him not. And He is the Most High, the Tremendous! (Al-Baqarah 2: 255). Such is Islam's concept of God, the first and foremost article of faith for every Muslim. It places Godhead in a position above and beyond all limitations. God alone is the Creator and Moulder, the Bountiful and the Forgiver, the Giver and the Withholder, the Just Ruler and the Great Avenger, the Omniscient and the All-Knowing, the Master of His bondsmen's destinies, the Cherished and the Wise.

This powerful and all-embracing monotheism forms the basis of all the religious, moral and social teachings of Islam. From the principle of God's Oneness and Uniqueness flows His sole creating power. He is the Originator and Fosterer of the Universe, the Fount of All Life-giving grace and the One to whom man is ultimately responsible. He Alone is worthy of worship and praise. The attribute of God's Unity and Transcendence leads on to His measureless Mercy and Nearness to man. Being the Most Gracious, He rears, sustains and fosters everything from its inception to its final perfection. (Al-Fātiḥah 1: 2). The benevolence of God bridges the gap between man and his Creator. He ordains: *"Pray unto Me and I will hear your Prayer."* (Ghāfir 40: 60). He is closer to His creations than their jugular veins. (Qāf 50: 16). He requires no property and no sustenance from His creation. (Adh-Dhāriyāt 51: 57). Nor does He need trustees, deputies or mediators. Belief in the Unity of God is accompanied and attended by a sense of impeccable justice and fair play. The believer cannot be tyrannical, because God is Just and Merciful; he cannot be a liar or deceiver, for he has to render account to the Omniscient God who knows stealthy looks and that which the breasts conceal. (Ghāfir 40: 19). He cannot show partiality to anyone since all men stand equal before the Lord; and, because Allah acts in this way, the believer must imitate his Master in dealings with his fellow beings. Faith in One God purifies the soul of the believer from evil and wickedness for he no longer exists for himself but for all his brethren in God's creation.

Prophethood

The second article of faith of which Islam raises its edifice is Prophethood or the guidance vouchsafed to man through Divine Messengers and Apostles. God has, in His Mercy, provided for all the known and unknown needs of man, the vicegerent of God on earth. He has also endowed man with all the capabilities required to unravel the secrets of physical laws in order to requisition these to his advantage. A little reflection reveals that nothing which man needs for his existence on this earth has been left unprovided for. But man needs something else too: he wants to know his Creator, His attributes, the purpose of creation and the meaning of life itself, for he cannot lead a life that is without purpose or direction. The continuous quest of man for truth since his advent on this earth, the disquietude of his soul bears witness to this fact. So, has God left man to grope in the dark alleys of uncertainty with regard to his most cardinal need? Obviously, this cannot be so.

Islam affirms that an order of Prophethood has been raised by God in every age and in all parts of the world (An-Nisā' 4: 164) to explain the true nature and attributes of the Lord and Master, to guide man to the virtuous path in the eyes of his God, and to unfold the meaning and purpose of his life on earth. But all these teachers of humanity were no more than mortals (Ibrāhīm 14: 11), none of them shared the attributes of Divinity nor did they possess any power to benefit or harm anybody save as Allah willed. (Al-A'rāf 7: 188). They were, thus, inspired teachers of humanity, the bearers of good news and warners (Al-An'ām 6: 44), who followed that which was revealed to them. (Yūnus 10: 15). Islam, therefore, enjoins the faithful to believe in all the Apostles of God without making any distinction between any of them. (Al-Baqarah 2: 285). It declares unequivocally that Muslims are those who believe and observe the teachings of Divine Apostles in thought as well as in deed (An-Nisā' 4: 64), for the Messengers of God brought the Truth (Al-A'rāf 7: 43); obedience of the Prophets is obedience of God; revolt against the Prophets is rebellion against God (Al-Aḥzāb 33: 36); and that Divine torment will afflict those who deny the Revelations vouchsafed to God's Messengers. (Al-Mā'idah 5: 49).

Islam also tells us that the underlying thought and content of the teachings of all the earlier Prophets of God was one and the same: their Revelations differed only in detail; this because of the time and circumstances in which they were revealed and man's capacity to understand them. However, the ministry of the last Prophet (peace be upon him) put a seal on earlier Revelations. Muhammad (peace be upon him) was sent as the Apostle of God for the last era which superseded the guidance brought by earlier Prophets. The Revelation brought by him not only included and confirmed all earlier Revelations, it also amended, improved and perfected their teachings and vouchsafed the final version of Divine Guidance to mankind to meet his requirements till the end of time. (Al-Aḥzāb 33: 40).

The Hereafter

Belief in resurrection after death and in the Day of Judgement is another essential ingredient of the Islamic creed. All the earlier Prophets demanded a belief in the Hereafter, for its denial means rejection of God as the Lord of the Day of Judgement. Nay, its denial renders belief in God and Prophethood meaningless. God is Beneficent and Merciful, no doubt; but He is also Just. He has full and unfettered authority to pardon or punish anybody He pleases. Still, justice demands that the virtuous and the sinner should not be placed on the same plane. In fact, the world with all its vices and virtues is too limited a place to requite the virtuous and evil-doers in full measure. There must, therefore, be another existence to dispense justice to both these categories. The Hereafter is, thus, of basic importance to a religion like Islam which demands belief in the existence of God and His attributes, the principle of Prophethood and Revelation through it. The Islamic creed, accordingly, not only demands belief in the world to come and resurrection of the dead on the Day of Judgement, but also warns wrong-doers of a dreadful penalty and promises blissful joys and pleasures to the pious and virtuous. The Qur'an says that God has not created man for nothing: nor were the heavens and earth and all that is between them created playfully. (Al-Dukhān 44: 38). Man should never think that he is to be left aimless. (Al-Mu'minūn 23: 115). It poses the question of whether God will treat those who believe and do good work in the same way as those who spread corruption on earth. (Al-Qalam 68: 35). It then emphatically declares that Allah has created the heavens and the earth with Truth, and that every soul will be repaid what it has earned; and it shall not be wronged in that. (Al-Jāthiyah 45: 22).

A Well-defined Creed

This is a good opportunity to review a distinguishing feature of Islam, or, for that matter, of all the Semitic religions. Just as it is often difficult for a Christian or a Muslim to understand the flexibility of approach on the part of Indo-Aryan religions manifested in their individualistic quest for the Ultimate Reality, the Hindus, Jains, or Buddhists go amiss by the elaborate dogma, the creed, canons and religious observances of Semitic religions which, to them, bespeak of their intolerance.

Every candid reader of the revealed scriptures, the Old and the New Testaments and the Qur'an would surely be impressed by the fact that the outlook of the Apostles of God has been dominated and wholly transformed by consciousness of the Lord and Creator of the World. The impact of His Person upon their thought and lives has been one of complete loyalty and obeisance to the Will and Pleasure of God, and a faithful transmission of the guidance vouchsafed to them. In all these religions, it is claimed that the revealed literature is a Sacred Scripture and, as such, constitutes the community's rule for faith and conduct. The concern or *raison d'être* of all these Scriptures, therefore, is exact interpretation of the Law with its manifold regulations and ordinances. The slightest deviation from the well-defined path chalked out by these Scriptures is taken as defiance of the Divine ordinances and condemned as impious and irreligious. Islam for its part takes extra care to maintain its original teachings – the Scripture as well as the creed and observances. It has, indeed, for this very reason, succeeded in preserving its original form and content more meticulously than can be claimed by any other religion. It might be added here that the concern of all Semitic religions, particularly of Islam, to preserve its originality and identity arises out of their sincere belief in the truthfulness of Divine Revelation rather than because of any intolerant zeal or obstinacy.

There is no denying the fact that a Muslim is committed to a particular ideology and honestly considers it superior to all other ideologies. By the very nature of this commitment, he is forced to consider his ideology alone as rightly correct. If tolerance means to believe that all religions are right and that all finally lead to the same goal, that is, to the Ultimate Reality, then, Islam, undoubtedly, does not subscribe to their view. As already stated, it teaches that it alone is right, as declared by the Qur'an unequivocally in the following verses:

> *"Lo! religion with Allah is Islam (surrender to His Will and Guidance)."* (Āl 'Imrān 3: 19).

> *"And who so seeketh a religion other than Islam (surrender to Allah), it will not be accepted from him, and he will be a loser in the Hereafter."* (Āl 'Imrān 3: 85).

This attitude of Islam is, in very truth, a necessary outcome of its clear, correct and sincere thinking. It presents before humanity an incontrovertible fact that human intellect is capable of owing allegiance to only one ideology at a time. The following verse of the Qur'an succinctly brings out the same truth in its inimitable manner:

> *"Allah hath not assigned unto any man two hearts within his body."* (Al-Aḥzāb 33: 4).

But this does not mean that the Muslim is intolerant of the beliefs of other people; his commitment to Islam requires him to tolerate not only other peoples' rejection of his own ideology, but also to accept it as their legitimate right to do so. Islam concedes equality to members of all faiths; for, it declares the universal rule that *"for you is your religion, and for me is my religion."* (Al-Kāfirūn 109: 6). In another place the Qur'an says: *"There is no compulsion in religion."* (Al-Baqarah 2: 256). Islamic Law guarantees not only freedom of conscience, performance of religious rites and inviolability of the places of worship of non-Muslims but also their right to have their personal matters regulated in accordance with their own religious and personal laws. Thus, the conviction in the truthfulness of Islam does not produce a blind or unreasoning adherence to the faith or a spirit of partisanship for fellow Muslims; nor does it smack of the slightest injustice to followers of other religions. *"God commands justice and good doing,"* (An-Naḥl 16: 90) says the Qur'an and also enjoins that: *"when you voice an opinion, be just, even though it be against one near of kin."* (Al-An'ām 6: 152). The Holy Prophet of Islam (peace be upon him) strongly condemned all chauvinistic ideas; national, linguistic and racial prejudices and passions of hate and aggression engendered by narrow sympathies in these words: "He is not one of us who gives a call for partisanship, he is not one of us who fights for partisanship and he is not one of us who dies for partisanship."[2] The insistence of Islam on its revealed character, for these reasons, does not countenance bigotry, prejudice or intolerance to other faiths in any shape or form.

Religious Observances

Four religious observances, known as the four pillars of Islam, are incumbent on every Muslim who has come of age and is in possession of sound mental faculties. These include the observance of ritual Prayer (*namaz* or *salat*) five times a day, payment of the poor-due (*zakat*) once a year provided one is liable to pay it, keeping the fast (*rozah* or *saum*) during the month of *Ramadan* and pilgrimage (*hajj*) to the House of God (Ka'bah) once in a life-time. These are the religious duties enjoined by Divine Revelation. Anybody denying faith in the dogma, in one or all the ritual observances, or omitting their observances permanently is deemed to have lapsed from the faith and the Muslim community.[3]

One may not be liable to pay the poor-due (*zakat*) or perform the pilgrimage (*hajj*) if certain conditions[4] laid down by the religious Law of Islam (*Shari'ah*) are not fulfilled, but no exception is made in the case of an adult and sensible man so far as the observance of ritual Prayer (*namaz*) and keeping the fast (*rozah*) are concerned. However, if a man is sick enough that the fast is likely to aggravate his illness or if he fears that it will cause hardship during the journey undertaken by him, he may defer it for the time being. He has to make up the omission as soon as the disability requiring its postponement is removed. Prayer, on the other hand, is to be punctiliously observed in all circumstances, whether one is in camp or on the march, confined to bed or in good health, for it should never be missed by a Muslim. As soon as the time for Prayer arrives, everything else is to be forgotten except man's duty to God. The only concession allowed is that if one is unable to stand, the Prayer can be performed sitting, lying or even in gestures; but the duty must not be neglected, not even on the battlefield.[5] However, when one is travelling one can offer two *rak'ats* of such obligatory Prayers as consist of four, and forgo other categories of Prayers which are then to be treated as purely voluntary.

The ritual Prayer (*namaz*) is, thus, by far the most important obligatory religious observance of Islam, constituting the mark and symbol of a Muslim and the line of demarcation between Islam and un-Islam.

The Times Fixed for Prayers

As already mentioned, Prayers are to be offered five times a day. These are known as *fajr* (morning), *zuhr* (meridian), *'asr* (afternoon), *maghrib* (sunset) and *'isha* (night).

The time for the *fajr* (morning) Prayer begins at the appearance of true dawn[6] and lasts till sunrise; the *fajr* Prayer is offered during this period. The Prayer consists of four *rak'ats*, two of which are offered individually and then the other two in congregation. As the time for *fajr* is ideally suited for Prayer, the recitation of the Qur'an in this orison is a bit longer than that in other Prayers. The Prayer is preceded by a call to Prayer before dawn with the addition of a sentence, repeated twice, saying: "Prayer is better than sleep." This is a reminder to Muslims, young and old, to get up and begin preparations for the performance of their obligation to God. The two-*rak'at* non-obligatory Prayers known as *sunnah*,[7] exceed merit and are offered before the obligatory (*fard*) Prayer. No Prayer can be offered after the completion of the obligatory Prayer of *fajr* until the sun rises.

The time for *zuhr* (meridian) Prayer commences as soon as the sun has begun to decline from its zenith and remains until an object throws a shadow twice its size.

The period of *'asr* (afternoon) Prayer lasts from the time prescribed for the *zuhr* Prayer comes to an end till sunset. It is better to offer *'asr* Prayer before the sun loses its brilliance.

The time for the *maghrib* (sunset) Prayer commences immediately after the sun has set till evening twilight totally disappears. It too ought to be performed immediately after sunset.

The last Prayer of the day, vis., *'isha* (night) orison can be offered after the time for *maghrib* Prayer expires until the dawn of the next day, but it should preferably be offered before midnight.

In all, the five obligatory Prayers consist of 17 *rak'ats*:[8] two of *fajr*, four each of *zuhr*, *'asr* and *'isha* and three of *maghrib*. In addition to these obligatory Prayers, one has also to offer twelve *rak'ats* of *sunnah* Prayers and three of *wajib*[9] Prayer of *'isha*.

The distribution of *sunnah* Prayers is: two *rak'ats* at *fajr*; six at the time of *zuhr*, four before the obligatory Prayer and two after it; two after the *fard* Prayer of *maghrib*, and two intervening the obligatory and *wajib* Prayers of *'isha*. The *wajib* Prayer of *'isha* is also known as *witr*.

The *sunnah* Prayers mentioned here are of a class which the Holy Prophet of Islam (peace be upon him) used to offer regularly and which he also insisted his followers perform. Standing third in order of merit after the *fard* (obligatory) and *wajib* (essential) Prayers, these too are not to be missed without some very cogent reasons.

How the Prayer is Performed

Now let us see how the Prayer is performed by the Muslims and what they recite in it standing, kneeling, sitting and in prostration. We will also describe how it is begun and terminated. There is hardly a man in India or any other country of the world where Muslims reside, who has not heard the call to Prayer or not seen Muslims offering Prayers, but very few will be conversant with its meaning and content. Indeed, many people have only vague ideas about the Muslim way of worship since they have never bothered to ask about it from their Muslim friends and neighbours.[10]

The Call to Prayer

First, let us take the *adhan* or the call to Prayer. There is hardly a city, town or village in India with a mixed population of Hindus and Muslims where the echo of this call is not heard five times a day. We give here both the Arabic words and their meanings as people are generally conversant with the call but not with its purport.

Allahu Akbar (four times)	Allah is Most Great.[11]
Ash-hadu al-la-ilaha illallah (twice)	I bear witness that there is none worthy of worship except Allah.
Ash-hadu anna Muhammadar-Rasoolullah (twice)	I bear witness that Muhammad is the Messenger of Allah.
Hayya 'alas-Salah (twice)	Come to Prayer.
Hayya 'alal-Falah (twice)	Come to success.
Allahu-Akbar (twice)	Allah is Most Great.
La-ilaha illallah	There is no deity but Allah.

Ablution

Muslims prepare for Prayer by performing ablution or *wudu'* which is essential for ritual purification. The worshipper should not only be in a state of legal purity in his person and clothes, he should also go through the ritual of *wudu'* before performing his duty to God. For this he has to wash his hands up to the wrist, gargle to cleanse his mouth, rinse his nostrils, wash his face from the forehead to the chin bone and from ear to ear, and the forearms up to the elbows. He then passes his wet hands over his head and follows by washing his feet up to his ankles. Every act is repeated three times. Prayers fixed for more than one time can be performed if the state of ritual purification is maintained, which, however, is nullified by calls of nature and sleep, etc. The mosques normally have arrangements for the performance of ablution. It is however, preferable to set out for the mosque after performing the ablutions. In some of the larger mosques water-taps are provided and arrangements are also made for the supply of hot water during the winter season.

The Prayer

Immediately after reaching the mosque, or after performing the ablution, if needed, one engages in voluntary Prayers, *sunnah* or a *nafl*, or in recitation of the Qur'an, or else recollection of God. In any case, one silently awaits the start of the congregational Prayer, for it is strictly forbidden to talk about the affairs of the world in the mosque. As soon as the *Imam*[12] takes his place to lead the congregational Prayer the *adhan* is repeated again, although not as loudly, with the addition of the words: "*Qad qamatis-Salah, Qad qamatis-Salah* – Prayer has indeed begun; Prayer has indeed begun." This second call to Prayer is known as *Iqamah*. The *Imam* always stands at the front in the centre, with rows of the faithful ranged behind him facing the Ka'bah.

Now, everybody hastens to join the congregation. If need be, even voluntary Prayers are curtailed. The *Imam,* who is normally a religious teacher or a *hafiz* or an educated person,[13] raises both his hands up to his ears and then, saying *Allahu Akbar,* brings them down and places his right hand upon the left below the navel. The whole congregation then follows suit after repeating the intention (*niyat*) to offer that particular Prayer. This intention is essential to the validity of the Prayer since Islam insists on the importance of the element of conscious will in every act of worship to God. The Prayer begins with an entreaty, offered silently by the *Imam* as well as his followers which runs as follows:

> "All Glory be to Thee, O Allah!
> And Praise be to Thee:
> Blessed is Thy Name and Exalted Thy Majesty;
> And there is none worthy of worship besides Thee."

Still standing, the *Imam* follows this with recitation of *Surah Fātiḥah,* the first chapter of the Qur'an, either silently or aloud.[14] This is the *Surah* recited in every Prayer since it contains the 'opening or essence of the Divine Writ': oft repeated on several occasions, it is the fount of Divine grace and blessing. The English rendering of this chapter of the Qur'an is:

> *"In the name of Allah, the Beneficent, the Merciful.*
> Praise be to Allah, Lord of the Worlds,
> The Beneficent; the Merciful.
> Owner of the Day of Judgement,
> Thee (alone) *we worship; Thee* (alone) *we ask for help.*
> Show us the straight path.
> The path of those whom Thou hast favoured;
> Not (the path) *of those who earn Thine anger*
> nor of those who go astray." (Al-Fātiḥah 1: 1–7).

The recitation of *Surah Fātiḥah* is ended with *Ameen.*"[15] The *Imam* then recites one or the other shorter *Surahs* or a few verses from any chapter of the Qur'an. The meanings of the two smaller *Surahs* are given here by way of illustration:

Surah al-'Aṣr (Time Through the Ages)

> "*In the name of Allah, the Beneficent, the Merciful.*
> By the declining day,
> Lo! man is in a state of loss,
> Save those who believe and do good works,
> and exhort one another to truth and exhort one another to endurance." (Al-'Aṣr 103: 1–3).

Surah al-Ikhlāṣ (The Unity)

> "*In the name of Allah, the Beneficent, the Merciful.*
> Say: He is Allah the One!
> Allah, the eternally Besought of all!
> He begetteth not nor was begotten.
> *And there is none comparable unto Him.*" (Al-Ikhlāṣ 112: 1–3).

The recitation from the Qur'an having finished, the *Imam* inclines the upper part of his body, repeating *Allahu Akbar*, and places the palms of his hands on his knees in obeisance to God. Everyone follows the *Imam* and they recite: "All glory be to my Lord, the Great." The *Imam* and the congregation stand up for a short while, the *Imam* reciting: "Allah has listened to him who has praised him"; while the congregation responds, saying, "Our Lord, praise be to Thee." The *Imam* again recites the formula, "*Allahu Akbar*" and falls to the ground along with the entire congregation with their foreheads on the ground, to say: "All glory be to my Lord, the Most High." If the kneeling (*ruku'*) signified honour to God, the prostration (*sajdah*) reminds the worshipper that he is but dust and nothingness before his Creator and Sustainer. The worshippers now raise their heads and sit down for a few seconds, then they again fall to the posture of the greatest surrender to Allah as if the first prostration (*sajdah*) had not satisfied their hearts and souls. Each movement is marked by the recitation of *Allahu Akbar*, while praise of God is repeated during the second prostration. Having thus completed the first *rak'at*, the *Imam* and the congregation stand up to repeat it once again for the second or subsequent *rak'ats*. After every two *rak'ats* the worshippers sit down after the second prostration to beseech God to bestow peace on them and the Holy Prophet (peace be upon him). They recite:

> "All reverence, all worship, all sanctity are due to Allah. Peace be on you, O Prophet, and also the Mercy of Allah and His Blessings. Peace be on us and all the righteous servants of Allah. I bear witness to the fact that there is none deserving of worship except Allah and I bear witness to the fact that Muhammad is His servant and Messenger."

If the Prayer is to be terminated after this *rak'at*, the worshipper continues sitting to invoke Divine Blessings on the Prophet Muhammad (peace be upon him), who brought the Divine Message to him, in the manner that God blessed earlier Prophets:

> "O Allah! Shower Thy Blessings on Muhammad and his descendants[16] as Thou showerest Thy Blessings on Abraham and his descendants. Verily, Thou art the Praiseworthy, the Glorious.
>
> O Allah! Bless Muhammad and his descendants as Thou blessedest Abraham and his descendants. Verily, Thou art the Praiseworthy, the Glorious."

And, then:

> *"Our Lord! Give unto us in the world that which is good and in the Hereafter that which is good, and guard us from the doom of Fire."* (Al-Baqarah 2: 201).
>
> "O Allah! Save me from the tribulation of Hell and from the affliction of the grave. O Allah! I seek refuge in Thee from the trials of life and death and from the scourge of *Dajjal*, the false Messiah.

To end the Prayer, the *Imam*, followed by the congregation, turns his face to the right and then to the left, saying: "Peace and grace of God be upon you."

The Prayer must be recited in Arabic.[17] Its brief outline is given here to acquaint non-Muslims with the manner and content of the Muslim's way of worship, for most of them have only a vague idea about it.

The Friday and *'Id* Prayers

On Friday, the *zuhr* or meridian Prayer is replaced by a congregational Prayer of two *rak'ats*, which cannot be offered alone. The Prayer is preceded by a sermon (*khutbah*) and unlike the *zuhr* Prayer, it is recited aloud. Friday is the weekly holiday of Muslims when a bath of general purification (*ghusl*) and the donning of washed garments are recommended in preparation for the Friday Prayers.[18] It is also considered meritorious to offer this Prayer in the chief mosque of the city. One such mosque, known as a *Jame' Masjid*, can be seen in almost every large city as, for instance, the *Jame' Masjid* of Delhi or Agra, where Muslims congregate in large numbers every Friday spotlessly attired. On reaching the Mosque, they first offer a few *rak'ats* of voluntary Prayer and then wait silently for the sermon (*khutbah*) to be delivered by the *Imam*.

The Friday Sermon

Normally, the Friday Prayer is held only in one of the town's mosques but in large cities where the congregation is too big to be accommodated in a single mosque, the Prayer is held in several mosques. Every such mosque has a pulpit (*minbar*) to the right of the central arch (*mihrab*), or a wooden structure (resembling a small platform with a few steps) used by the *Imam* or preacher (*khatib*). As soon as the preacher takes his place on the pulpit (*minbar*), a second call to Prayer is proclaimed by someone standing a short distance in front of the *khatib* or *Imam*. The sermon ought to consist, as the Prophet (peace be upon him) used to deliver them, of an exhortation to follow the precepts of Islam, elucidation of the fundamental tenets of faith and a discourse on any important matter worthy of inviting the attention of the faithful on this solemn occasion. The orations delivered by the Prophet (peace be upon him) on Fridays were always of moderate length but eloquent and forceful. In certain Islamic countries, particularly those which have Arabic as their mother-tongue, every Friday-sermon is a new exercise in oration but in India and other non-Arabic speaking countries the *khutbah* is normally read out from any printed collection of Friday sermons. Sometimes the *Imams* commit the *khutbah* to memory to be rehearsed on each Friday.

The *khutbah* delivered on Fridays consists of two parts: the first, relating to the main sermon and, the next, invoking blessings on the Holy Prophet (peace be upon him), his Companions and others. The two parts are delivered by the preacher with a short break between. The *khutbah* is normally delivered in Arabic but preachers have begun addressing the congregation in their mother-tongues between the Arabic invocation at the beginning and end of the sermon.

The *khutbah* given here is indicative of the Friday sermons usually preached in India. It is taken from a popular collection[19] of orations from which the sermons are read out by most *Imams* nowadays.

> "(After the praise of God and invocation of blessings on the Prophet Muhammad) O ye people, accept Divine Unity (in His Being and Attributes and associate no partner unto Him), for that alone constitutes the supreme act of submission to God and the greatest piety. Be meek and crestfallen before God, for surrender unto Him is the fount of all virtues. Follow in the footsteps of the Holy Prophet (on whom be the peace and blessings of God), for the way of the Prophet leads you to submission to God; and, whoever obeys God and His Messenger, he shall be guided on the straight path and reach his destination. Shun innovations in religion, since these will lead you astray to the path of disobedience to God and waywardness. Adopt truthfulness, for veracity brings life and falsehood means death. Let charity and kindness be the guiding principles of your life, for Allah loves those who are gracious to others. And never lose hope of the mercy of God, because He is the Most Merciful of all the merciful ones. O ye people, do not be enamoured of the world, lest you should lose whatever you have. You shall not quit the world unless you have had everything destined for you; then, why this vain effort for accumulating wealth through illegal and wrongful means and by transgressing the limits set by God, Exalted is He. Adopt legitimate and lawful means to achieve your ends and pin your faith in God, for He never disappoints those who place reliance on Him. Never be weary of supplication, as He listens to those who call Him. Always seek forgiveness for your sins as this will attract Divine blessings and increase your wealth and progeny. God says in the Qur'an: "*And your Lord hath said: Pray unto Me and I will hear your Prayer. Lo! those who scorn My service, they will enter hell, disgraced.*" (Ghāfir 40: 60).

Allah may help all of you and me too to gain understanding of the Holy Scripture and to benefit from the wisdom contained therein. I seek forgiveness from God for you as well as for all the believers; you should also seek refuge in Him from evil desires and sinful actions. Verily, He is the most Merciful, the Forgiver of sins."

This is the first part of the *khutbah*. The second part consists of an invocation of the peace and blessings of God on the Holy Prophet, the rightly-guided Caliphs, the members of the Prophet's household, and all Muslims, and normally it is concluded with this verse of the Qur'an:

> *"Lo! Allah enjoineth justice and kindness, and giving to kinsfolk, and forbiddeth lewdness and abomination and wickedness. He exhorteth you in order that ye may take heed."* (An-Naḥl 16: 90).

The Friday Prayer

The *khutbah* being ended, the preacher descends from the pulpit. If he also officiates as *Imam* he takes a position in front of the congregation and leads it in a two-*rak'at* Prayer. Thereafter, the worshippers offer a few more *rak'ats* of *sunnah* Prayers and then disperse to look after their interests. This is what the Qur'an requires as it entails no obligation of a weekly rest like the Jewish Sabbath or the Christian Sunday. The Qur'an says that *"when the Prayer is ended, then disperse in the land and seek of Allah's bounty."* (Al-Jumu'ah 62: 10).

Tahajjud Prayer

The Prayers of the two *'Ids* have already been described along with fairs and festivals. Of the other important Prayers, one is that of *tahajjud* which, although a voluntary Prayer, has been so emphatically emphasised by the Holy Prophet (peace be upon him) as well as by the Qur'an for the development of conscious devotion and spirituality that certain doctors of faith have been led to hold the view that this Prayer was obligatory for the Prophet of Islam (peace be upon him). Many devout Muslims, perhaps more in India than in other Islamic countries, get up in the dead of night to establish communion with their Lord. They can be seen offering eight or twelve *rak'ats* of this nocturnal Prayer, immersed in the remembrance of God, seeking nearness to Him, begging His favour and bowing in thanksgiving unto Him so as to make self surrender and obeisance to Him the ruling passion of their lives, finally culminating in love – love that satisfies the yearning of the human heart. *Tahajjud* Prayer is offered in units of two *rak'ats* in each of which normally the longer chapters of the Qur'an are recited. The time for *tahajjud* begins after midnight and lasts till day-break.

Zakat

Zakat or poor-due is the second important observance or pillar of the edifice of Islam. The Qur'an mentions it over 30 times, along with Prayer which ranks top-most among obligatory religious observances and describes it as an insignia of submission to God.

Zakat is payable by every adult Muslim of sound mental condition, provided he owns estate or effects exceeding a certain minimum value called *nisab* which varies for different items. In other words, *zakat* is payable by a believer if he owns in addition to his own requirements, various categories of possessions exceeding the *nisab*. For example, the *nisab* fixed for gold is seven and a half *tolas*[20] and fifty-two and a half *tolas*[21] for silver. If someone has remained in possession of these metals for one complete year, i.e. these have been with the owner in excess of his requirements, he is liable to pay one fortieth (two and a half percent) of it by way of poor-due. Merchandise of the same value is liable to be similarly taxed. For the fruits of the soil (agricultural produce), one-tenth of the annual harvest is payable, but a twentieth part is to be paid if the cultivation requires costly irrigation. The number and kind of cattle composing flocks and herds determine the varying rates of *zakat* for each category. *Zakat* is paid once a year and is spent on the poor and the needy.[22]

Zakat: Not a Tax but an Act of Worship

Zakat, in Islam, is not a tax or a levy designed merely to solve monetary problems, but rather a Prayer, an act of worship necessary for spiritual and moral betterment and gaining propinquity to God. Like other religious observances, therefore, an intention (*niyat*) to pay the *zakat* is essential. Alms given without the intention to pay the *zakat* are as ineffective as a Prayer offered without it.[23] *Zakat* is not to be paid by the believer vaingloriously but humbly and unassumingly with downcast eyes. One who pays the *zakat* should himself search out the poor and the needy and thank the person accepting it for his co-operation in the performance of his religious duty. The religious ordinances relating to *zakat* attach more merit to the distribution of *zakat* collected from the rich amongst the poor of the same place (except where no such persons are to be found there). Muslim law prohibits lending on interest. It places the two, interest and *zakat*, in balance, one exceeding in merit and virtue to the same extent as the other engenders impiety and covetousness.

Charity and Almsgiving

Zakat signifies merely the lowest limit of the legally incumbent almsgiving by a believer in possession of wealth and property in excess of the *nisab*. Even after paying *zakat*, he still remains liable to help the poor and the needy and to spend in the way of God for all these have a share in his earnings. *Zakat* thus marks the beginning and not the end of charity. At the same time, Islam does not recognise any particular class or caste to whom the *zakat* or other charities should be paid as a matter of right. It has, on the other hand, permanently debarred *Bani* Hashim, i.e. the clan and descendants of the Prophet (peace be upon him), from accepting anything of *zakat*, and has, thus, put a check on economic exploitation on the basis of religion.

Rozah: The Third Obligatory Observance

Fasting (*rozah*) is the third fundamental observance, obligatory like Prayer (*namaz*), on every adult Muslim not insane or suffering from any other disability. A sick person or a traveller may abstain from fasting but he has to make up for the omission by keeping the fast on an equal number of days in any other month. The fast lasts a full lunar month during *Ramadan*, the ninth month of the Muslim year, in which the first Revelation of the Holy Qur'an was made to the Prophet (peace be upon him). It is a month of Divine blessings and great spiritual merit.

Ramadan: A Month of Rejoicing

Ramadan begins with the sighting of the new moon and brings with it an aura of spiritual bliss in Muslim localities, mosques, hearths and homes. A spirit of rejoicing, pulsating with new life and spiritual emotion fills people, young and old. *Ramadan* is, undoubtedly, a month of abstinence and self-restraint, strict discipline and self denial but its arrival is hailed as an occasion of the greatest joy. More time is spent during *Ramadan* in Prayer and recitation of the Qur'an and the number of worshippers in the mosques increases manifold. There is also considerable addition to *'isha* Prayers with the sighting of the *Ramadan* moon, but people make a point of finishing their business in good time to join the evening and night congregations.

Tarawih

During the month of *Ramadan,* 20 additional *rak'ats* performed in units of two each, are offered after night Prayers. These are called *Tarawih.* This special Prayer is accompanied by recitation of the entire Qur'an during the course of Prayers, i.e. after *Surah Fātiḥah* in each *rak'at.* Recitation of the entire Qur'an at least once in these Prayers is a must, but in certain mosques it is repeated five or six times during the month. Instances are not lacking where the *Imams* recite half or even the entire Qur'an in a single night! The *Tarawih* Prayers normally take an hour or two but sometimes these may last till dawn.

Sahri

It is customary to take a "dawn meal" an hour or so before day-break in order to gain strength for the fast. This is called *sahur* in Arabic and is known as *sahri* in India. The practice has the sanction of the Prophet who exhorted his followers to observe the custom. Indian Muslims usually add variety to their meal on these occasions, if their means permit. The "dawn meal" must be finished before the call for morning *(fajr)* Prayer is announced. Normally, people take care to finish the *sahri* even before its time comes to an end.

Fasting

Now, with the twilight of dawn appearing on the horizon, the *rozah* begins with the *niyat* or intention: "I intend to fast for this day for the sake of Allah in the month of *Ramadan*." This has to be expressly repeated.

The fast (*rozah*) enjoined by Islam differs from the fasts kept on grounds of health or those prevalent among the followers of other religions. During the fast, it is forbidden to eat or drink anything from dawn to dusk, and the rule is strictly observed even when *Ramadan* occurs in midsummer. Not only is there total abstinence from food and drink of all kinds, without any distinction, but even smoking or taking of medicines, fruit juice or the like is also prohibited. The fast is not broken if anything is taken unintentionally but voluntary violation of the fast must be paid for by 60 days of continuous expiatory fasting.

Zeal for Worship and Prayer

The arrival of *Ramadan* is marked by the increased zeal for voluntary Prayers and remembrance of God, and, particularly, by recitation of the Qur'an. Every believer keeping the fast makes it a point to recite a portion of the Qur'an every day. *Ramadan* also awakens the spirit of charity, benevolence and generosity: the Holy Prophet (peace be upon him) called it a month of kindness and benefaction when the merit of that given in charity is increased 70 times by God.

A Month of Self-discipline

Ramadan not only combines fasting, Prayer and charitableness but also enjoins abstinence from falsehood in speech and action, slander, libel, lying, lustful looks, ill-will against others, etc. All these vices prohibited by Islam become a greater sin during this month. The Holy Prophet (peace be upon him) is reported to have said: "Allah does not require anybody to abstain from food and drink if he does not give up lying and deceitful action."

Iftar

Suddenly a cannon shot or a lighting signal on the top of the minaret of a mosque or the call to evening Prayer announces that the time to break the fast has arrived. The believer hastens home or to the mosque to take a light meal called *Iftar* with the supplication on his lips: "O Allah, for Thy sake have I fasted, in Thee have I faith and I break the fast with the food that comes from Thee." Verily, the fast was kept for the sake of God and so has it been broken at His bidding, and, therefore, the believer must not have his fill unless he has offered his thanks to God for its successful completion. He takes a few morsels of food and joins the *maghrib* congregation before taking the evening meal.

Dates are especially valued for breaking the fast during *Ramadan*; emulation of the practice followed by the Prophet of Islam (peace be upon him) has an additional merit in every spiritual or mundane affair. After the whole day's abstinence from food and drink, the recovered liberty in the evening finds expression in the variety of dishes prepared for the *iftar* and the evening meal. Indian Muslims usually have some very tasteful preparations, especially of grams, which are not found in other Muslim countries.

Khatm-i-Qur'an

The daily life of a Muslim is adapted to a new cycle of engagements during the month of *Ramadan*. The major portion of his time, from *iftar* to the time he goes to sleep is taken up by night Prayers and *Tarawih,* as stated elsewhere. Every Muslim considers it his bounded duty to listen to the recitation of the whole Qur'an at least once in *Tarawih*. For this purpose, some people join those *Tarawih* congregations where the recitation is completed in five or seven days and then offer these Prayers by themselves. Resort to such devices is taken by those not sufficiently strong in faith; but what expedients are not managed by the indolent to meet the arduous requirements of religion and law! In India there is a custom of decorating the mosques and distributing sweets, normally on the twenty-seventh night or thereabout, when recitation of the Qur'an in *Tarawih* is completed. The occasion is known as *Khatm-i-Qur'an*.

I'tikaf

The traditions assert that the Prophet (peace be upon him) used to spend the last ten days of *Ramadan* secluded in his mosque in Prayer and remembrance of God. It is naturally considered virtuous to follow the practice of the Holy Prophet (peace be upon him). A number of orthodox Muslims, accordingly, retire to the mosque on the evening of the twentieth day of *Ramadan* and emerge after the new moon of *'Id* has been sighted. During this period, known as *i'tikaf*, one can come out of the mosque only to satisfy nature's calls, but *wudu'* and similar other permissible acts are to be performed within the bounds of the mosque. *I'tikaf* signifies that one has left the affairs of the world, one's home and dependants, for ten days to devote oneself exclusively to the worship and recollection of God. Fasting, coupled with intensive Prayer and meditation, away from the cares of the world, during the period of *i'tikaf*, affords an opportunity for spiritual development and prepares the worshipper to suffer the greatest privation and the hardest trial for the sake of his faith.

Shab-i-Qadr

Just as greater merit is attached to the last days of *Ramadan*, there is *Lailatul-Qadr* or the 'Night of Power' which is 'worth more than a thousand months.' (Al-Qadr, the Power 97: 3). The Qur'an has a chapter named after it. Revelation from God came down to earth in the month of *Ramadan* and, more exactly, on the Night of Power, which has, however, not been specified by God. It might be the 21st, 23rd, 25th, 27th or 29th night of *Ramadan* but the 27th night is considered more probable. This night is spent in vigil and Prayer by orthodox Muslims.

The New Moon of *'Id*

The month of fasting and Prayer, restraint and self-discipline comes to an end with the sighting of the new moon of *'Id*. *Ramadan* is bidden goodbye with a heavy heart. The joy of the coming *'Id* mingles with the sorrowful gloom felt for the departing *Ramadan* and, with it, the blessings of the Lord. If it was considered sinful to take any food or drink any water during *Ramadan*, it would now be sacrilegious to abstain from lawful foods and drinks on the day of *'Id*. The moral is clear to Muslims: all virtue and merit, piety and sanctity depend on an unflinching submission to the Will and Pleasure of the Creator and Lord of the Worlds.

Hajj

Hajj is another religious duty incumbent on every true Muslim if he has the means[24] to make the pilgrimage to Makkah. Islam attaches so much importance to the institution that a Muslim is liable to be declared an apostate, in accordance with the injunctions contained in this regard in the Qur'an and the Traditions, if he possesses the means but does not perform the *hajj*. The pilgrimage is performed with certain fixed rites at Makkah, which are gone through from the 8th to the 12th of *Dhil-Hijjah*, the last month of the Muslim lunar year.

The Rites of *Hajj*

As already stated, the ceremonies of *hajj* have to be performed on the sacred precincts of Makkah and the two neighbouring places, Mina and 'Arafat, on fixed dates. These ceremonies being an integral part of the pilgrimage, and having been specified by Holy Scripture and the practice of the Prophet of Islam (peace be upon him), cannot be performed at any other place or on any other date. The Muslim tradition connects it with the two most venerable Prophets of God, Abraham and Ishmael, who, when commanded by their Lord, willingly laid their lives at the altar of God. It was at these places, on these very days that the father and son, with concerted will, came out successful from the supreme trial of self-sacrifice in the service of God. It was indeed a great and arduous trial to test the love and affection, ardour and devotion of the two men whose ennobling example will ever continue to inspire mankind and inflame their hearts with Divine love. The commemoration of this noblest sacrifice accompanied by the repetition of the rites performed by these two Apostles of God allows believers, on the one hand, to partake the spirit of adoring affection for God felt by them and, on the other, links them all, belonging to different countries and nationalities, in the common heritage of Abrahamic belief and culture and the way of his life. The pilgrimage, of a fact, has been the greatest factor in preserving the religious and cultural solidarity of Muslims the world over by forging a common link between them as well as with the centre of Islam, the House of God.[25]

It would be out of place to describe in any detail the rites performed at the time of *hajj*. These rites are fairly long and consist of numerous details which can be seen in the writings of

Muslim legists, and can be understood only by undergoing all these rituals under the guidance of experts known as *mutawwif*. Here we shall try to accompany the intending pilgrims in order to give a broad idea of the way *hajj* is performed.

Travel for the Pilgrimage

Indian Muslims are known for their genuine feelings of religious enthusiasm for the *hajj* and their number exceeds that of any other country where Muslims are in a minority. There is great rejoicing when the pilgrims set out from their villages or towns for the *hajj*; they are given a send-off with the most distinguished marks of respect; friends and relatives beg them to remember them in their invocations to God at the holy places and wish them success in their journey. Elderly *Hajees* entertain a subconscious wish to die on the sacred soil of the holy cities. With this end in view, it is customary for pilgrims to take with them a shroud which they bring back dipped in the water of Zamzam, to be used as a burial garment when they ultimately give up their soul.

Engagements at the Port

At ports of embarkation where pilgrims have normally to spend a few days before the ship begins its journey, pilgrims can be seen studying the rites of the pilgrimage. Those who are educated try to gain acquaintance of the geography and historical importance of the places they are to visit. Normally the pilgrims engage in pursuits which may be helpful in the performance of the *hajj* and in deriving the maximum benefit from the journey undertaken at considerable cost and inconvenience. In the ships too, arrangements are made for daily discourses on the *hajj*, its importance and the ceremonial rites connected with it in order to keep the hearts of the pilgrims smitten with the love of God.

Ihram

When the ship carrying the pilgrims from India reaches Yalamlam, a siren is sounded to inform the pilgrims that it is the place where they should put on their special pilgrim garments (*ihram*). This is the *miqat* for pilgrims coming to Makkah from the south. There are different *miqats* for people coming from different directions, the farthest being those coming from Madinah. It also signifies that the pilgrim should prepare himself mentally as well as in his outward appearance and attire for presenting himself before the Lord of the Worlds.

Pilgrims take a bath for ritual purification and change into two seamless white sheets of cloth. Women do not have to put on the pilgrim's garment (*ihram*) but they cannot now cover their faces until the *hajj* is completed. They offer a two-*rak'at* Prayer and express the formal intention (*niyat*) of performing the *hajj*. Now they have to abide by all the regulations prescribed for the *hajj*; the clothes they had been wearing are now prohibited; they must now be bare-headed and must not cover their heads and faces; and, finally, they must remain in these special shroud-like clothes till the day of the great sacrifice on the tenth day of *Dhil-Hijjah*. Now no distinction remains: young and old, rich and poor, white and black, all wear the same garments. Even the different languages spoken by the pilgrims hailing from different parts of the world is obliterated for everyone has the same song of love on his lips:

> "Here I am at Thy service, O Allah!
> Here I am at Thy service;
> Here I am at Thy service;
> There is no partner unto Thee;
> Here I am at Thy service;

To Thee belongs all praise, the riches and the sovereignty of the world.
There is no partner unto Thee."

The ship resounds with the chanting of the faithful who are now lost in the ecstasy of love for the holy land and its Lord. Henceforth, marital relations, mutual acrimonies, insolent behaviour and abusive language – all are prohibited and remain a grievous sin until the pilgrim's garment (*ihram*) is taken off. The Qur'an ordains: *"Whoever is minded to perform the pilgrimage, therein there is (to be) no lewdness nor abuse nor angry conversation on the pilgrimage."* (Al-Baqarah 2: 197).

Some of the pilgrims appear to be restless; while others seem to be lost to the world – in an unearthly sea of happiness. For some the journey is the first of their life and what a journey, towards what an exalted goal! It has been their life-long wish to see the holy city, once, even if they had to die after it. They have always offered Prayers, facing the inviolable House of God, never slept with their feet on the side of the Ka'bah nor answered the call of nature facing that direction; and, now, this goal of their life is so near!

The Ka'bah

And lo! the pilgrims find themselves, suddenly, within the limits of the Haram.[26] Fast-moving vehicles take the pilgrims to the Holy Mosque. Now they are within the inner square of the sanctuary with its large cube about forty feet high, covered with black brocade with a broad band of gold embroided verses from the Qur'an running around the upper portion of the covering. At its southeast corner, the Black Stone (*Hajar al-Aswad*) surrounded by a silver frame is embedded in the wall which has been kissed hollow by many generations of pilgrims simply because this only remnant of the original House of God built by Abraham was kissed by the Holy Prophet (peace be upon him). This then, is the Ka'bah: without any definite ornamentation, without any structural beauty of line and form; it stands in utter simplicity, as man can conceive of no architectural beauty befitting the Lord, Most High.

There is indescribable joy when pilgrims first see the Ka'bah, the goal of their longing. A few seem to be in a state of delight, some shed tears of joy while there are still others who are dumbfounded as if captivated by the glory of God before their eyes. Now, the pilgrims walk round the Ka'bah seven times, kiss the Black Stone and offer Prayers facing it from any side they desire. There are also the hillocks of Safa and Marwa, at a short distance, which mark the places between which Hagar ran seven times in search of water for her little Ishmael. Her frantic search for water was so liked by God that every pilgrim must now traverse the track, in imitation of Hagar, increasing and slowing his paces like her, for the *hajj* is not complete without undergoing this *sa'ee.*

In the Plain of 'Arafat

It is now the eighth day of *Dhil-Hijjah.* Pilgrims proceed to Mina, some four miles out of Makkah and camp there. On the ninth morning, they proceed to 'Arafat, about eight miles further on. Here, they fulfil the basic demand of the pilgrimage of *hajj*, for this is the ceremony of ceremonies to be performed during the pilgrimage. But, after all, what is this rite? Recollection of God for the whole day, repentance over one's past sins, a cry of anguish in the form of *labbaik*, *labbaik*, and a solemn promise to lead a virtuous, pious life in future!

The Supplication at 'Arafat

We give here the supplication once offered by the Prophet of Islam (peace be upon him) in the plain of 'Arafat, and now repeated by pilgrims to express their renunciation and self-surrender, humility and helplessness on this solemn occasion.

> "O Allah!
> Thou hearest what I say;
> Thou seest where I am;
> Thou knowest what I keep secret and what I express. Nothing that I do remains concealed from Thee. I am an afflicted and helpless and a distressed soul. I seek Thy refuge for I am appalled and horrified. I acknowledge my mistakes, my sins;
> and I implore Thee like one forsaken and forlorn;
> I cry to Thee as one humiliated and abased;
> I call upon Thee as one miserable and crushed;
> I fall on my knees like one whose head hangs in shame before Thee, whose eyes shed tears, who has thrown himself at Thy feet and is crouched before Thee. O Allah! cause me not to fail in supplicating before Thee. Thou art Most Gracious and Most Merciful for me. Verily, Thou art the Best of all who are implored, the Most Bountiful of all givers."

This is the plain of 'Arafat; a city of tents: no houses, no buildings; people of all races and languages clad in the all-equalising *ihram*, beseeching God, shedding tears; sobbings and murmurings fill the air. When acquaintances meet, they exchange greetings, people eat and drink, but all are burdened by the care to atone for their past sins and prepare for a virtuous life henceforth. The Prayers of *zuhr* and *'asr* have been performed at their appointed times and it is now the time for *maghrib* (sunset) Prayer: this orison has been performed throughout one's life exactly at the time fixed for it, but today it has to be offered late at Muzdalifah, for there is no virtue in any Prayer offered by force of habit or of one's own accord – the merit lies in doing what God ordains, the Prayer is for Him and all are His slaves.

Back to Mina

As soon as the sun goes down, a cannon shot sounds the warning to leave the plain of 'Arafat. The tents are at once rolled up and the thronging crowd moves on to Muzdalifah, a distance of about six miles. The pilgrims again halt to take rest for the night and proceed early next morning to offer supplications at Mash'ar-i-Haram. They pick up pebbles from here to cast at the stone pillars that represent the Devil. This is the rite called *rami* (*al-Jamrat*), reminding one how Abraham had rejected the promptings of Satan to dissuade him from sacrificing his only son in the way of God. Now they again return to Mina. The pilgrims had left it when the Master had so desired and now they wend their way back to it at His call. Obedience towards God is the essence of all customs and rituals; of the *hajj* itself.

The pilgrims remain at Mina for three or four days. On the 10th of *Dhil-Hijjah* they stone the Devil, offer the sacrifice and then circumambulate the Ka'bah at Makkah. This circumambulation is the most important and more meritorious than all those performed before or after. The pilgrimage proper is now over, and the *hajees* wash and shave and change into their ordinary clothes. The pilgrims must, however, spend three days at Mina. On the next two or three days they must stone the stone pillars that represent the Devil again. No other rituals now remain and the pilgrims are free to pay social visits, make friends with Muslims hailing from the far-flung world of Islam and create bonds of mutual understanding and common weal.

In the City of the Prophet

The pilgrims are now impatient to pay a visit to Madinah, if they have not already done so on the upward journey. It is not incumbent, only meritorious, to betake oneself to Madinah; nevertheless, who can deny that but for the beloved Messenger of God, on whom be blessings and peace, there would have been no circumambulation of the Ka'bah, no *namaz*, no *hajj*! One is naturally anxious to make one's salutations to the greatest benefactor of humanity, offer Prayers in his mosque which increases their merit fifty thousand times, see the houses and the lanes and the paths where the Prophet once lived, walked and preached, and witness the land on which are still visible the imprints of the sacrifices and achievements of the Prophet (peace be upon him) and his Companions.

Having completed the *hajj*, the pilgrims return to their homes. This is again an occasion for rejoicing in the towns or villages at the safe return of the pilgrims. Neighbours make a point of paying congratulatory calls on returning pilgrims, who, for their part, bring small presents for friends and relatives. It may be a rosary, a few dates or a bottle of Zamzam water, but even the poorest pilgrim will bring back his modest little gift purchased in the city of *Bait Allah* (House of God) for his friends.

This is how the *hajj*, the fourth most important duty incumbent on every Muslim possessing the means is performed. The pilgrim is now entitled to be known as a *Hajee*. Prayer (*namaz*), fasting (*rozah*) and the poor-due (*zakat*) are all incumbent on him as ever, as on other Muslims, but he is now burdened with an additional responsibility to prove himself worthy of the honour conferred on him by the new title attached to his name.

NOTES

1. Apart from oneness, i.e. being one, single or individual, the word unity in English also denotes being formed of parts that constitute a whole.

Accordingly, God, the Holy Spirit and the Son of God constitute Godhead in the Christian dogma. Quite apart and opposed to this view, the Unity or *Tawhid*, according to the Islamic concept, recognises no partners and associates whatsoever in the Unity of God.

2. Abu Da'ud.
3. For a fuller explanation of these four religious duties and their meaning and purpose see *The Four Pillars of Islam* by the author, published by the Academy of Islamic Research and Publications, Luknow.
4. For details see any book dealing with religious observances.
5. The manner in which Prayer is observed on the battlefield can be seen in a book of *fiqh* dealing with ritual observances.
6. Before dawn, a streak of whiteness first appears in the eastern sky which is followed by a brief spell of darkness. Thereafter, the whiteness of daybreak again appears and goes on increasing till the sun is visible.
7. Any observance expressly ordained or having the sanction of the Prophet's practice.
8. A *rak'at* is a unit of Prayer consisting of recitation of the Qur'ān in a standing posture, genuflexion and two prostrations.
9. *Wajib* is a Prayer which ranks next to the *fard* or obligatory Prayer.
10. The writer of these lines has had some very interesting experiences in this connection. Once, when he was performing a congregational Prayer with some friends during the course of a railway journey, a Hindu traveller who appeared to be well educated asked whether we meant the Moghul emperor Akbar by '*Allah-o-Akbar*' repeated frequently in the *namaz*! Another friend of mine was asked a similar question by a Hindu professor of a certain university. These incidents show how little we know of our neighbour's religious beliefs and observances.
11. Allah has been retained here as there is no corresponding word in English. The word Allah (the stress is on the second syllable) has neither feminine nor plural, and has never been applied to anything other than the unimaginable Supreme Being.
12. One who leads the congregational Prayer.
13. Islam does not recognise any priestly order for leading the Prayer or performing other religious functions. Any Muslim having adequate knowledge about the observance can perform it. However, the *Imams* as well as the *mu'adhdhins* (those who give the call to Prayer) are appointed in certain mosques and paid for by the community with the object of their proper management.
14. The Qur'ān recited audibly in the first two *rak'at* of *fajr*, *maghrib* and '*isha* as well as in the Friday and '*Id* Prayer.

15. Meaning, accept our invocation, O Allah.
16. The word *'Aal'* in Arabic, which is translated here as 'descendants', also includes in a wider sense the followers.
17. The directive that the Prayer (*namaz*) be performed in Arabic alone has been of the greatest value in preserving the original form of worship and has also saved the Muslims from falling prey to parochial and linguistic differences in religious observances. A Muslim can perform the Prayer, thanks to it being offered in Arabic, in any mosque in any part of the world led by a Muslim not speaking his own language.
18. This does not mean that Muslims only take a bath on Fridays. Its frequency depends, for obvious reasons, on the climatic conditions of any particular place as well as the customs and habits of the people. Many Muslims take a bath every day, or on alternate days, but the bath on Fridays, being founded on the precept of the Prophet of Islam (peace be upon him), is supposed to carry additional merit.
19. Compiled by Maulana Muhammad Isma'il Shahid Dehlawi (d. 1246/1830).
20. Equivalent to 37.5 grams.
21. Equivalent to 612.4 grams.
22. This statutory alms (*zakat*), of which only the general principle has been summarised here, is one of those chapters of Islamic jurisprudence (fiqh) on which voluminous treatises have been written. At the time of writing, we have before us a copy of *Fiqh-uz-Zakat* by Shaikh Yusuf al-Qaradawi of Egypt, published recently, and which covers 1,131 pages across two volumes. In a book written to introduce the basic Islamic tenets no more detail could possibly be given. Those who are interested to know further about it might refer to *The Four Pillars of Islam* by the current author.
23. *Rasail-i-Arkan* by Maulana Bahr-ul-Uloom Firangi Mahalli, p. 163.
24. One has to possess not only the means to undertake the journey but should also leave enough for the maintenance of one's dependants during one's absence. In addition, the pilgrim should be in good health, to undertake the journey.
25. The innumerable details of these rites of pilgrimage cover a larger part of the writings of Muslim jurisprudence. It is in fact one of the most difficult parts of Muslim religious law and extensive treatises exist on the subject, some of which have been written by Muslim scholars of India. Of the most authoritative and exhaustive works on *hajj*, *Zubdatul Manasik* by Maulana Rashid Ahmad Gangohi, *Umadatul Manasik* by Maulana Sher Muhammad Sindhi and *Mu'allimul Hujjaj* by Mufti Sa'eed Ahmad occupy pride of place.
26. The limit around Makkah demarcating the sacred bounds of the holy city begin about 24 or 25 kilometres from the city.

VI

A FEW CHARACTERISTICS OF THE MUSLIMS

A distinguishing feature of the entire Muslim community, including Indian Muslims, is that the fundamental basis of their existence as a religious community (*millat*) is a well-defined, distinct and immutable faith and a Divinely-ordained canon (*Shari'ah*). Like other prevalent systems of faith and worship, Islam too is a religion, no doubt, but the word hardly expresses the true nature of Islam and, furthermore, causes it to be misunderstood if only owing to its general usage by all the other faiths indiscriminately.[1] It is for this reason that instead of deriving its name from any race, clan, country or founder of the religion, it calls itself man's self-surrender (Islam) to God. This self-surrender expresses itself not only in belief in God but also in duteous obedience to His commands. It bespeaks, also, of the fundamental difference between the followers of Islam, who are called Muslims, and the adherents of other faiths who get their names from the founders of their religion, the place of their origin or a race or a clan. The Jews are also known as Judaists and *Bani Israel* or Israelites: Judah was one of the sons of Prophet Jacob who was himself called Israel. Christians draw their name from Jesus Christ while one of their earliest names, Nazarenes or its Arabic form (*Nasara*), as mentioned in the Qur'an, is derived from Nazareth, in Galilee, the home town of Jesus Christ.

Zoroastrians, known as *Parsees* in India, get their name from the founder of their religion, Zoroaster or Zarathustra. The same is the case with Buddhists, named after Gautama Buddha, and this is so with almost every other religion.

The Muslims

Believers are called in the Qur'an, religious treatises, historical books and literary compositions, either *Muslimoon* or *Ummat-i-Muslimah*, and they are still known throughout the world wherever they reside by the name of Muslims. As already explained, the name is a derivative of Islam, "the surrender" to Allah, embracing certain defined principles, ideas, values and criteria for the guidance of humanity. Despite their ardent love and attachment to the Holy Prophet of Islam (peace be upon him), Muslims have never agreed to their being called Mohammedans. It was the British who first nicknamed them Mohammedans and their religious law (*Shari'ah*) as Mohammedan Law. But the Muslims protested against the name given to them by their erstwhile rulers and preferred to be known as Muslims. Certain institutions[2] which had been named as Mohammedan College or Mohammedan Conference during the early phases of British rule in India had to be changed later on under the pressure of Muslim public opinion about the unsuitability of the word 'Mohammedan.'

The Content and Form of Faith

The reason for this strong public opinion which might appear as of trivial importance to certain people is that the form of faith is as important from the Muslim viewpoint as the content itself. The faith as well as its manifestation in the form of religious law (*Shari'ah*) are of basic importance for the uniqueness of the Muslim culture and its way of life. There is, indeed, no basis in

Islam for the notion that the Islamic *Shari'ah* is just another code to be obeyed, as we dutifully obey the laws of a city or a state. It represents the sense of the believers' absolute responsibility to the Will of God, and for that reason, it has to be spelled out in detail for the guidance of the faithful. It is, thus, not at all surprising that Muslims are so sensitive regarding any talk about so-called reforms in Islamic Law. This is a matter of paramount importance for Muslims which ought to be taken into account in chalking out a course of action in any individual, social or national matter affecting the Muslims.

It has also to be borne in mind that except for a few local customs, usages and conventions which somehow found their way into the body of laws recognised as Mohammedan Law during British rule in India, the Muslim Personal Law rests upon the Qur'an, as interpreted through and expanded by the rules of Muslim jurisprudence (*fiqh*) on the basis of the sayings and confirmed practice (*ahadith*) of the Prophet of Islam (peace be upon him). To be sure, the Qur'an lays down the rules, sometimes in great detail, for the fundamental institutions of Muslim social life, such as personal behaviour, morals, marriage, inheritance and economic activity. Where only general principles are laid down, these are supplemented by another authoritative source, the *hadith*, or spelt out by Muslim doctors of religion on the basis of the probable action of the Prophet (peace be upon him) and his Companions in the light of Qur'anic precepts. Thus, the authority and validity of Muslim Personal Law is derived from the belief that they conform to the Will of an All-controlling God rather than social experience or rational speculation.

Inviolability of the *Shari'ah*

This brief elucidation of the nature of Muslim Personal Law shows that those laws which have been laid down in explicit and unambiguous terms in the Qur'an and which have been acted upon by the Muslim community without any interruption so far, are inviolable and immutable. These are unalterable, mandatory provisions of Islamic Law and anybody transgressing these rules would be deemed, according to the consensus of Muslim doctors of faith, an apostate and outcast of the Muslim community. There may be differences of opinion among Muslim doctors with regard to the interpretation and practical application of these mandatory laws, but there has been absolutely no question, nor is there now, of any reform or change in these Qur'anic Laws. No Muslim State nor any elected legislative body has any right to interfere in these laws, and any effort in that direction should be construed as interference in the practice of religion.

There are, however, other laws, as pointed out earlier, which comprise matters for which there was either no clear guidance, rule or injunction available in the Qur'an or the *ahadith* or those which fall in the category of non-prohibited matters, and which were spelt out later on by Muslim legists in conformity with the spirit of the Islamic *Shari'ah*. In these matters, the doors of difference of opinion and interpretation about the best course of action in the light of the general principles and precepts of the *Shari'ah* as well as the changing needs of the times, have always been open in the past, are open even today, and will continue to remain so in the future. Muslim doctors of faith and jurisprudents having profound legal knowledge and a developed sense of interpreting matters in the true Islamic spirit can interpret the rules falling in the latter category in the light of changed circumstances and the needs of present-day life. This process of assimilation and interpretation has always been operative in the past and will remain so in the future.

Taharat

Another unique feature of a Muslim's personal life arises out of his singular concept of personal and external purity. It demands, apart from general cleanliness, a state of legal purification too which is very often not understood by non-Muslims. Cleanliness denotes freedom from dirt or stain both in one's person and clothing. Legal purification (*taharat*) goes further and demands that one should be free from every defilement, great or small, like excretion, urine, wine, blood, the saliva of a dog, dung, etc. in the smallest quantity. Thus, however free from dirt a man may be and however stainless his dress, a speck of any defilement renders him legally impure and disqualifies him from offering Prayers. Similarly, if anyone has not washed his private parts after excretion or urination or requires to take a bath (*ghusl*) owing to any defilement,[3] he cannot attain purification without proper bathing. The repast, utensils, table-linen, clothing, bed-linen and all other articles of daily use should likewise be free from every defilement in addition to their being clean or free from dirt.

Dietary Restrictions

Another characteristic of the Islamic teachings having a profound impact on the Muslim's way of living is the distinction it makes between prohibited and permissible articles of food. The Qur'an does not leave its followers free to eat whatever they like but lays down a clear line of demarcation between the two types of foodstuffs which should not be overstepped by any Muslim.

In the case of animals and birds whose flesh can be eaten, they must be immolated in the name of God. The flesh of any animal that has been dedicated or offered in sacrifice to an idol or a saint or a person considered to be 'divine' or a martyr is strictly prohibited, and such is the case with the animal that meets a natural death or dies owing to injuries received in hunting before it is sacrificed in the name of God. The swine has been declared desecrate and defiled and its flesh detestable, while there are other animals which are not profane but their flesh is prohibited. Lions, tigers, panthers, dogs and similar other feline and carnivorous beasts as well as all hunting birds and those birds which use their claws in eating fall into the prohibited category. Such dietary restrictions constitute a distinguishing mark of the Abrahamic way of life: his tastes and taboos, likes and dislikes were, in truth, confirmed by God as Divine injunctions to regulate the culinary practices of the Muslims of every country and every age till the end of time.

Indian Muslims too have abided by these regulations and, to an extent, more meticulously than their co-religionists in many other Muslim countries. They are more cautious, law-abiding and sensitive with regard to Divine commandments than the Muslims of certain other countries whose faith has been enfeebled by the ever-increasing impact of the materialistic civilisation of the West and sudden opulence. Almost similar is the case with wine which has ever remained prohibited in the eyes of the *Shari'ah*. Muslims have known it as the "mother of all evils," and never allowed it to gain a foothold in Muslim society. In the use of alcoholic liquors too, the behaviour of Indian Muslims has been more in keeping with the demands of the *Shari'ah* than that of certain Westernised Muslim countries.

Love of the Prophet

The Muslims' intense attachment to the Prophet of Islam (peace be upon him) is another distinguishing feature of their lives. The Prophet (peace be upon him) is not simply the founder of the faith, or a venerable personage but something more than that: a tender feeling of heart-felt love and respect for the Prophet (peace be upon him) is what a Muslim treasures more than anything else. A Persian poet expressed the same feeling in these words, which cannot perhaps be surpassed:

"Ba'd az khuda Buzurg Tu'ee Qissa Mukhtasar"
"To cut short, most respected thou art after God."

At the same time, Muslims have been expressly asked to desist from exaggerated adulation and deification of the Holy Prophet (peace be upon him) as was done by the followers of certain earlier Prophets. A tradition of the Holy Prophet (peace be upon him) says: "Do not extol me beyond my limits nor entertain exaggerated notions about me like the Christians who unduly magnified their Prophet. Call me, if you have to, by the name of the slave and Messenger of God."

Unparalleled Love and Affection

In spite of the restraining effect of moderation preached by Islam in praising the Prophet (peace be upon him), the heart-felt love and the deep attachment the Muslims have for him is unparalleled and unsurpassed by the followers of any other religion for their Prophet or the founder of their faith. It can rightly be claimed that millions of them revere and love the Prophet (peace be upon him) more than their own lives, their children and parents and are ever willing to sacrifice their all to guard his honour. The sensitiveness of the Muslims in this regard has been demonstrated on countless occasions and can still call forth supreme sacrifice from them. The Muslims cannot suffer the slightest disparagement of their beloved Prophet (peace be upon him) in any shape or form. Even today the Prophet's name, his honour, his city, his sayings and his teachings and anything connected with him arouse the tenderest feelings of love and fervour of devotion for him. The following lines by the late Maulana Zafar 'Ali Khan, a poet and editor of the daily *Zamindar* of Lahore, adequately express the ardent love Muslims have for their Prophet.

> "The *namaz* and *zakat* and the *rozah* and *hajj*, virtuous are all;
> But a Muslim I am not despite these all;
> Unless for the honour of Madinah's chief, I gladly give up the life I have.
> By God, short of that, imperfect shall ever remain my faith!"

The never-ending Divine blessings invoked for the Prophet of Islam (peace be upon him) day in day out, the merit and virtue of these benedictions, the large number of the Prophet's biographies written by the Muslims of India[4] and of other countries and the eulogies composed by poets to adore and pay their respects to him, speak of the deepest love and regard entertained by the Muslims for the Messenger of God (peace be upon him). It is worth mentioning here that the eulogium has always remained, in every language, a melodious medium to express the sentiments of gratitude to a benefactor, but the ode to praise a particular personage, for whom every poet deems it an honour to sing praises, is essentially a product of the Muslim mind. If nothing similar to it is found in the poetry of other peoples, it is because no other personage has been held in a similar esteem and regard by his people. The eulogies in praise of the Prophet of Islam (peace be upon him) in almost every language spoken by the Muslims have a place of their own in those literatures if only on account of their literary merit, rhythmical creation of beauty, exquisite expression and the warmth of feeling contained in them. Excluding Iran which has had some of the best eulogist poets, the contribution of Indian Muslims to this form of poetry is without parallel in any other language spoken by Muslims. Some of the well-known poets of the Indo-Pakistan subcontinent who have indited eulogies of exceptional poetic beauty, sublime in thought and artistic in construction, in the praise of the Holy Prophet (peace be upon him) are Mohsin Kakorwi, Amir Minai, Khawaja Altaf Husain Hali, Maulana Zafar 'Ali Khan, Dr. Sir Muhammad Iqbal, Iqbal Ahmad Suhail and Hafeez Jalandhari. An eulogist poet, Aasi Ghazipuri, has beautifully summed up the feelings of love and respect felt by Indian Muslims for the Prophet of Islam (peace be upon him) in these words:

> "Convey my *Salam* and tell him (the Prophet), O Zephyr,
> After the remembrance of God, thee alone we revere."

The Finality of Prophethood

It is an article of faith for Muslims that Muhammad (peace be upon him) was the last Messenger and the seal of all the Prophets. No Revelation shall ever descend on a man after Muhammad, and whoever makes such a claim shall be no more than a liar and a deceiver. This faith is grounded in the teachings of the Qur'an and the Traditions and the uninterrupted[5] belief of Muslims in this regard since earliest times. The conviction in the finality of Muhammad's Prophethood has been a citadel of safety protecting the faith of Muslims from falling prey to the artifices of clever renegades.

The Companions and the Prophet's Kin

Companion is the name given to a contemporary follower of the Holy Prophet (peace be upon him). Every Muslim acknowledges the yeoman's service rendered by each of them for the propagation of the Faith. They are all regarded as ideal Muslims, benefactors of humanity and pure-hearted souls worthy of the highest reverence. Whenever their name is mentioned, by any Muslim, he accompanies it with the phrase '*razi Allah 'anhu*' which means 'may God be pleased with him'. Four of the Prophet's Companions, viz. Hazrat Abu Bakr, 'Umar, 'Uthman and 'Ali who succeeded the Prophet (peace be upon him) as his rightly-guided Caliphs, are held in the highest esteem[6] and their names are mentioned along with the Prophet's in the orations (*khutbah*) of the Friday and *'Id* Prayers. In addition to these four Companions, there are six other pious followers of the Prophet (peace be upon him) who were given by him the glad tidings of redemption and Paradise. These are known by Muslims as the 'Promised Ten' (*'ashra'-i-mubashsharah*).

The members of the Prophet's household, known as *ahl-i-bait*, include his wives, daughters and the two grandsons, Imam Hasan and Imam Husain. Reverence and regard for each of these kin of the Prophet (peace be upon him) is deemed as a duty incumbent on all Muslims.

The Book of God

The same is the case with the Qur'an. It is not merely a collection of morals and tales of wisdom to be acted upon when convenient, but a Revelation from God, preserved word by word, for the guidance of humanity. It has suffered no interpolation, not even of a comma or a full-stop, since it was revealed to the Holy Prophet (peace be upon him). Muslims have been commanded to handle the Book reverently and perform ablution before reciting it.

All over the world there are a number of Muslims who have committed the entire Qur'an to memory. In India there are special types of schools which provide instruction in learning the Qur'an by heart and its recitation. Thanks to these schools,[7] India has hundreds of thousands of people who have memorised the whole Qur'an and some of them have attained such a high level of proficiency that they can recite the entire Qur'an in a single night. In fact, some of them do so every night during the month of *Ramadan*. It is not uncommon to see boys of 10 or 12 years of age who have learnt the voluminous Scripture[8] by heart. Nor are women[9] found lacking in this feat of memory.

Hadith and *Fiqh*

Next to the Book of God, Traditions (*hadith*)[10] and the rules of religious law (*fiqh*) have attracted the diligent attention of the Muslims. Traditions have been preserved with an unbroken chain of narrators from the Companions down to their Disciples and Successors till these were written down. A separate science for the verification and criticism of the Traditions was evolved which included the biographical account of all the narrators, their moral and spiritual worth, their memorising capacity and veracity. A large number of books, voluminous treatises and bibliographies, enough to fill a library, have been written on the subject. Indian Muslims have also given special attention to the science and produced some works of outstanding merit. During the last two hundred years, India has indeed been the centre of study and teaching of the Traditions, leaving all other Muslim countries far behind. Today, no Muslim or even Arab country can boast of the high standard of *ahadith* studies found in some Indian institutions, such as Darul Uloom Deoband, Mazahir Uloom Saharanpur, Nadwatul Ulama, Lucknow and Markazi Darul Uloom, Banaras. These institutions regularly graduate students in the science of the Traditions, carrying out research and bringing out valuable publications on the subject. They also have on their teaching staff doctors of exceptional merit and ability who must be the envy of other Islamic countries.

Islamic Brotherhood

Last but not least, the dominant trait of Muslim social life is its international brotherhood, a transcendental religious and spiritual affinity cutting across all barriers of race, language and nationality, to which a Muslim feels irresistibly drawn on account of his religious teachings. He, undoubtedly, loves the country to which he belongs; deems it an article of faith to defend its interests and lay down his life for its sake; but this does not stand in his way of taking an interest in the welfare of other Muslims whom he considers as members belonging to one and the same family. This concept of human brotherhood is like a celestial light that guides Muslims in the darkness of racial prejudice and national hatred: it teaches them to hate none but love all. Their interest in the affairs of other Muslims consists of a pious wish for their well-being, a feeling of sorrow for their misfortune, and moral support when they need it: this is in no way a stumbling block in the way of patriotism and love for their own country. They consider it a duty enjoined by justice and humanitarian ideals, embedded in their religion and a means of strengthening and furthering the interests of their own country.

Nothing bears out this assertion more clearly than the *Khilafat* Movement launched by Indian Muslims under the leadership of Mahatma Gandhi, The 'Ali Brothers Maulana Muhammad 'Ali Jawhar and Maulana Shawkat 'Ali, Maulana Abul Kalam Azad, Maulana 'Abdul Bari and other freedom fighters. The wonderful spectacle of Hindu-Muslim unity and the tremendous popular upsurge for the freedom of the country produced by the *Khilafat* Movement is still fresh in the memory of many a person in the country. The object of this Movement was to restore justice to the Turks and to preserve the *Khilafat* as much as to liberate their own country from the foreign yoke. The same political consciousness and feeling of sympathy for the Muslims of other countries has been responsible for the keen interest shown by Indian Muslims in the Palestine problem. There is no denying this concern of Muslims for humanity at large, and their co-religionists in particular: it is a characteristic of the Message of Islam which must be taken into account for a better understanding of the Muslims' attitude and behaviour.

NOTES

1. There are certain religions, for example Christianity, which owing to the impact of a repressive and totalitarian State in its formative stage, accepted the view best expressed by the Biblical adage: Render to Caesar the things that are Caesar's and to God the things that are God's. This, obviously, limits the sphere of religion to a few purely religious beliefs and practices – a private affair having hardly anything to do with the social aspect of human life. The religions of Indian origin, too, seem to consist of certain forms of worship and rituals as against a definite view of life and the world propounded by Islam. The word 'religion' as commonly applied to other religions is, thus, inadequate to convey the much wider sense conveyed by *Din* (the Path) as Islam calls itself.
2. Madrasatul-Uloom Aligarh, established by Sir Syed Ahmad Khan, was first known as the Anglo-Oriental Mohammedan College. When it was upgraded, its name was changed to Muslim University. Similarly the name of the once famous Mohammedan Educational Conference of Aligarh was also changed.
3. The *Shari'ah* makes a *ghusl* or bath obligatory after sexual intercourse, discharge or effusion of semen and completion of menses and confinement.
4. It is a matter of pride for Indian Muslims that their creations in the field of the Prophet's biographies have left the Muslims of other lands far behind. In the two-volume biography of the Prophet, *Siratun Nabi*, by Allama Shibli No'mani, four more volumes were added by his disciple Maulana Syed Sulaiman Nadwi. A few other works of repute are: *Khutbat-i-Madras* also by Maulana Syed Sulaiman Nadwi, *Rehmatul lil-'Alamin* by Qazi Muhammad Sulaiman Mansurpuri, *An-Nabi-ul-Khatim* by Maulana Manazir Ahsan Gilani and *Asahhus-Siyar* by Maulana Abdur Ra'uf Danapuri.
5. The uninterrupted transmission or *tawatur* of any act or saying means, in the phraseology of Muslim legists, that it has been acted upon and handed

down by an overwhelming majority, leaving not an iota of doubt about its authenticity.

6. The Shi'ahs differ in this respect from the Sunnis and consider only 'Ali as the rightful successor of the Prophet (peace be upon him).

7. Lucknow has a fairly large institution of this type known as Madrasa Furqaniah. It was established by Maulana Syed 'Ain-ul-Quzat (d.1925/1343) in 1908–9. Once, it attracted students from such far-off places as Afghanistan, Turkistan and Hijaz. Not able to maintain the same high standard, the institution is, nevertheless, still in existence. All other Oriental institutions teaching Arabic provide instruction in committing the Qur'an to memory.

8. The Qur'an is divided into 30 parts and 114 chapters (*surahs*) having 6,616 verses (*ayat*) of varying length with 340,740 letters. In a book of normal size printed in 16 point type of Arabic script it covers about 800 pages. Even children of even seven or eight years of age often commit the whole to memory.

9. In my own family, for instance, about a dozen women have learnt the entire Qur'an by heart.

10. Any saying or action attributed to the Holy Prophet (peace be upon him) and handed down by a reliable eye-witness through an unbroken chain of narrators.

Glossary

Allāhu Akbar: Allah is Great.
adhān: the call to Prayer.
aḥādīth: Traditions of the Prophet.
Alvadā': the last Friday of *Ramaḍān*, which in India is a festive day.
'aqīqah: a non-obligatory ceremony whereby seven days after a child's birth its head is shaved and a sacrifice is offered.
Ash-hadu al-lā-ilāha illallāh: I bear witness that there is none worthy of worship except Allah.
ashrāf: the higher strata in society.
'asr: obligatory afternoon Prayer.
assalam-o-'alaikum: the customary greeting meaning peace be upon you. The reply is *wa 'alaikum-us-salam*, on you be peace.

Baqra'īd: another name for the festival of *'Īd-ul-Aḍḥā*.
birādri: the endogamous social circle maintained by lower castes.
Bismillāh: the ceremony marking the beginning of a child's education. See also *maktab nashīnī* and *tasmia khwānī*.
Bismillāh-ir-Raḥmān-ir-Raḥīm: In the name of Allah, the Beneficent, the Merciful.

chālīswān: one of a number of special rites performed after death.

darūd: invocation of Divine blessings for the Prophet (peace be upon him).
Dhil-Ḥijjah: the twelfth month of the Islamic calendar.
Dīn: the Path or Islam, i.e. way of life.
Du'ā: supplication.

fajr: obligatory morning Prayer.
farḍ: something which is obligatory.
fiqh: Islamic jurisprudence.

Gayarahwin Sharīf: a special feast-day held in honour of the mystic saint Shaikh 'Abdul Qādir Jīlānī.
ghusl: bodily washing/bathing for general purification.

ḥāfiẓ: someone who has committed the Qur'ān to memory.
Ḥajar-i-Aswad: the Black Stone in the Ka'bah.
ḥājee: someone who has completed the pilgrimage to Makkah.
ḥajj: pilgrimage.
Ḥaram: the sacred bounds of Makkah.
Holi Milan: a Hindu festival.
hukka: a water-pipe.

'Īd-ul-Aḍḥā: the festival celebrated on the 10th day of *Dhil-Ḥijjah*, the last month of the Islamic calendar, when Makkan pilgrims gather at Mina to offer sacrifice, worship and recollection of God.
'Īd-ul-Fiṭr: the festival celebrated when the crescent moon is sighted at the end of the month of fasting, i.e. *Ramaḍān*.
'Īdgāh: an open place of worship where prayers for *'Īd-ul-Fiṭr* and *'Īd-ul-Aḍḥā* are offered.
Iftāri: the fast-breaking meal.
iḥrām: the garment worn by pilgrims.
ījaāb: offer, as in marriage.
Imām: someone who leads the Prayers.
imān: faith in Islam.
iqāmah: the second call to Prayer.
'ishā': obligatory night Prayer.
Islam: self-surrender to God.
I'tikāf: a period spent in the mosque in devotion and remembrance of God during *Ramaḍān*.

jahez: dowry gifts.
Jamrah: the place of stoning the Devil in Mina.
Jumu'at-ul-Wadā': the last Friday of *Ramaḍān*. See also *Alvadā'*.

Ka'bah: the house of God in Makkah.
kafan: burial shroud.
kalima-i-shahādat: the article of Muslim affirmation.
Kalimah: *Lā ilāha illallāh*; *Muḥammad ur-rasūl ullāh*: There is no God but God; Muhammad is the Messenger of Allah.
khaṭīb: preacher.
Khatm-i-Qur'ān: recitation of the entire Qur'ān.
khatnah: ritual circumcision.
khutbah: sermon.
kufw: the social equality of the partners in marriage ensuring the husband does not come from a lower stratum.

Lailatul-Qadr: the Night of Power which falls during *Ramaḍān.*
langar: public banquets.
laqab: surname.
lotā: a water jug with a specially shaped pipe used in performing ablutions.

maghrib: obligatory sunset Prayer.
mahr: dowry money.
maktab nashīnī: see *Bismillāh.*
Malik-ul-Mulūk: King of Kings.
maulood: lectures/sermons about the birth, life and teachings of the Prophet. See also *mīlād.*
mīlād: see *maulood.*
millat: religious community.
minbar: pulpit.
Mīqāt: Places specified by the Prophet (peace be upon him) beyond which a pilgrim from that side is not allowed to cross without *Iḥrām.* These places are: Yalamlam, for the pilgrims coming from Southern Asia like India, Pakistan, etc. Juḥfah (near Rābigh), for the people of Egypt, Syria, etc. Dhāt-'Irq, for the people of Iraq. Qarn al-Manāzil, for the people of Najd and Zul-Hulayfah (Abyār 'Alī), for the people of Madinah.
Mu'adhdhin: one who gives the call to Prayer.
Muḥarram: the first month of the Muslim year.
Muslimoon: Believers, i.e. Muslims. See also *Ummat-i-Muslimah.*

mustaḥab: a meritorious act which can earn reward in the Hereafter.
muṭawwif: expert guides to assist in the performance of *ḥajj* rites.

namāz: (*ṣalāt*) Prayers performed five times during the day.
namāz-i-janāzah: (*ṣalātul-janāzah*) funeral prayer.
nashrah: a simple ceremony performed after a child's first complete reading of the Qur'ān.
neuta: marriage gifts from relatives.
Night of Power: see *Lailatul-Qadr.*
nikāḥ: marriage contract.
niṣāb: the minimum value of one's estate from which *zakāt*, the poor-due, is calculated.
niyat: an intention expressed before offering Prayer.

Promised Ten: the Companions of the Prophet who were given redemption and a special glad tiding of Paradise. They are:

(1) Abū Bakr *aṣ-Ṣiddiq* ibn Abī Quḥāfah
(2) 'Umar ibn al-Khaṭṭab
(3) 'Uthmān ibn 'Affān
(4) 'Alī ibn Abī Ṭalib (the four rightly guided Caliphs), and
(5) Abū 'Ubaydah ibn al-Jarrāh
(6) 'Abdurraḥmān ibn 'Awf
(7) Az-Zubayr ibn al-'Awwām
(8) Sa'īd ibn Zayd
(9) Ṭalḥah ibn 'Ubaidullāh and
(10) Sa'd ibn Abī Waqqāṣ (may Allah be pleased with them all).

purdah: seclusion.

qabool: acceptance, as in marriage.
Qazi: judge or magistrate.
qiblah: the Ka'bah.
qiyām: a salutation sung in honour of the Prophet after the *mīlād.*
qul: see *chālīswān.*

Rajab: the seventh month of the Muslim calendar when a festival is held on the 27th to celebrate the Prophet's celestial journey through the heavens to God.

rajbi: a festival of Indian Muslim origin held during the month of *Rajab*.
rak'at: a unit of Prayer which consists of reciting the Qur'ān whilst standing, followed by genuflexion and two prostrations.
Ramaḍān: the month of fasting, ninth month of the Muslim calendar.
rozah: obligatory fasting, see also *ṣaum*.
rozah kusha'i: a special fast-breaking feast.
rukū': bowing in Prayer in honour of God.
rū-numāi: showing the face of the bride to the bridegroom after marriage.

sadqa-i-Fiṭr: the special charity of *'Īd* given after completion of *Ramaḍān*.
sahri: the dawn-meal taken during *Ramaḍān*, called *sahūr* in Arabic.
sajdah: prostration.
ṣalāt: the observance of ritual Prayer, see also *namāz*.
ṣalāt-i-tahajjud: night vigil, a voluntary nocturnal Prayer sanctioned by the Prophet.
ṣaum: see *rozah*.
Shab-i-Barāt: the festival held on the 15th of *Shaban*, the eighth month when God ordains all that happens to each individual in the following years.
Sharī'ah: Islamic Religious Law.
Sunnah: a saying or action of the Prophet considered exemplary.
Sūrah: a chapter of the Qur'ān.
surti: chewing tobacco, see also *zarda*.

tahārat: legal purification demanding that the Muslim be free from every defilement.
takbir "Allahu Akbar": the formula meaning Allah is Great.
tarāwīḥ: a special Prayer offered during *Ramaḍān* after *'Ishā'* Prayer.
tasmia khwānī: see *maktab nashīnī*.
Tawḥīd: the Unity of God.
tayammum: ritual dry ablution for Prayers when water for *wuḍu'* is not available.
tīja: see *chālīswān*.
tilak: dowry demands made by the bridegroom's family on the bride's parents.

'Ulamā': religious scholars.
Ummat-i-Muslimah: see *Muslimoon.*
Urs: a festival usually celebrating the birth or death anniversary of a saintly man.

wājib: a Prayer next in importance to a *Farḍ* obligatory Prayer.
walī: a guardian.
Wuḍū': necessary ritual ablution before offering Prayers.

zakāt: obligatory poor-due.
zarda: see *surti.*
ẓuhr: obligatory meridian Prayer.

Index

K

L

M

N

O

P

Q

R

S

T

U

W

Y

Z